TO DISPEL THE MISERY OF THE WORLD

Ga Rabjampa Künga Yeshé (1397–1470).
From the collection of Tharlam Monastery, Kathmandu.
Photo by Stefan Eckel.

To Dispel the Misery of the World

Whispered Teachings of the Bodhisattvas

Ga Rabjampa Künga Yeshé

Foreword by Khenpo Appey
Translated by Rigpa Translations

WISDOM PUBLICATIONS · BOSTON

Wisdom Publications, Inc.
199 Elm Street
Somerville MA 02144 USA
www.wisdompubs.org

Library of Congress Cataloging-in-Publication Data
Sga Rab-'byams-pa, 1397–1470.
[Byan chub kyi sems gñis bsgom pa'i man ñag bdud rtsi'i chu rgyun. English]
To dispel the misery of the world : whispered teachings of the bodhisattvas / Ga Rabjampa Künga
Yeshe ; foreword by Khenpo Appey ; translated by Rigpa Translations.
p. cm.
Includes bibliographical references and index.
ISBN 1-61429-004-0 (pbk. : alk. paper)
1. Bodhicitta (Buddhism)—Early works to 1800. 2. Spiritual life—Bka'-gdams-pa (Sect)—Early works
to 1800. 3. Bka'-gdams-pa (Sect)—Doctrines—Early works to 1800. 4. Ye-śes-rdo-rje, Chad-kha-ba,
1102–1176. Blo sbyon don bdun ma. I. Ye-śes-rdo-rje, Chad-kha-ba, 1102–1176. Blo sbyon don bdun ma.
English. II. Title.
BQ4398.5.S4313 2012
294.3'444—dc23
2011039566

ISBN 9781614290049
eBook ISBN 9781614290186

16 15 14 13 12
5 4 3 2 1

Cover photo: The bodhisattva Padmapāṇi in the Ajanta Caves, Maharashtra, India.
Reproduced with the kind permission of the photographer, Kunal Mukherjee
(web.mit.edu/~kunalm/Public).
Cover design by Phil Pascuzzo. Interior design by Gopa&Ted2.
Set in Diacritical Garamond Pro 11.75/15.

  This book was produced with environmental mindfulness. We have
elected to print this title on 30% PCW recycled paper. As a result, we
have saved the following resources: 10 trees, 4 million BTUs of energy, 1,036 lbs. of greenhouse gases,
4,672 gallons of water, and 296 lbs. of solid waste. For more information, please visit our website,
www.wisdompubs.org. This paper is also FSC certified. For more information, please visit www.fscus.org.

Dedicated to the memory of Khenpo Appey Rinpoche.

May his enlightened activity continue and

all his wishes be fulfilled!

Contents

Sogyal Rinpoche and Khenpo Appey Rinpoche
in Kathmandu, November 2008.
Photo by Stefan Eckel.

Foreword

⸙

Whoever wishes to afford protection
quickly to both himself and others
should practice that most holy secret:
the exchanging of oneself for others.

Thus said Śāntideva. Sakya Paṇḍita also said:

The exchange of oneself for others is said
to be the heart of Buddha's teachings.

As these verses suggest, the bodhicitta of exchanging oneself for others is
the swift path, the most holy secret, and the heart of the teachings. How
to put this into practice is the main focus of the *Seven Points of Mind
Training* by Chekawa Yeshé Dorjé, a disciple of the great Kadampa master Sharawa.

This book, *The Stream of Nectar*, is a clear and extensive commentary on these instructions by the learned Ga Rabjampa Künga Yeshé, a
famous disciple of both Ngorchen Künga Zangpo and Rongtön Shakya
Gyaltsen. In response to my suggestion that rendering this in English
would bring widespread benefit, Adam Pearcey has now accomplished
the task of translation, clarifying points of doubt with the great scholar
Zenkar Rinpoche Tudeng Nima and myself. It is my hope that this
will bring about the twofold benefit of both self and others for many

meritorious and fortunate individuals through the path of study, reflection, and meditation.

Khenpo Appey
International Buddhist Academy, Kathmandu, 2009

Preface

The late Khenpo Appey Rinpoche was among the most learned Tibetan scholars of recent times. Having studied with some of the greatest masters of the previous century, especially Khenpo Jamyang Gyaltsen, Dezhung Ajam Rinpoche, and Jamyang Khyentsé Chökyi Lodrö, he went on to become the tutor to His Holiness Sakya Trizin and other important teachers. His contribution to the teachings of the Sakya school was immense, and his legacy continues in the two institutes he founded, Sakya College in India and the International Buddhist Academy in Nepal.

Back in 2006, during an audience at his home in Nepal, our small translation group asked Khen Rinpoche if he could recommend a short, practical instruction that would be suitable for a general Western audience. Immediately, he offered us his very own copy of this text by Ga Rabjampa Künga Yeshé, which had only recently been published in Tibet. This is exactly what people of the modern world need, Khen Rinpoche told us emphatically—a manual on mind training, containing simple yet powerful instructions, especially on the practice of *tonglen*, or "giving and taking."

Over the next few years, whenever we visited Khen Rinpoche to update him on the progress of the translation and to ask questions, he was always incredibly generous, not only giving of his time to explain difficult points in the text but also, at one point, even offering to provide accommodation and financial support if needed.

In 2007, when Khen Rinpoche taught the *Seven Points of Mind*

Training at his International Buddhist Academy at the behest of Chökyi Nyima Rinpoche and the Rangjung Yeshe Institute, he used this text as a support for his explanation. Notes taken on that occasion, based in part on Thomas Doctor's lucid oral translation, have since proved invaluable.

The following pages include a version of the root text of the *Seven Points of Mind Training* extracted from Ga Rabjampa's commentary and, as far as possible, translated according to his interpretation. The main section of the book is the commentary itself, entitled *The Stream of Nectar*. Following this, we have included an aspiration prayer, taken from Ga Rabjampa's Collected Works, that is related to the *lojong* teachings and incorporates terms and expressions from the *Seven Points*.

Now that Khen Rinpoche has passed into *parinirvāṇa*, let this book be part of what the Tibetans call *gong dzok*, the fulfillment of a master's wishes and intentions.

TECHNICAL NOTE

The Tibetan text of Ga Rabjampa's commentary, entitled *Byang chub kyi sems gnyis bsgom pa'i man ngag bdud rtsi'i chu rgyun*, is found in volume 1 of Ga Rabjampa 2005: 152–282. It is WooEGS1016747 in the TBRC database. The aspiration prayer translated in the appendix, *Theg pa chen po'i blo sbyong gi smon lam byang chub lam bzang*, is found in the same volume, pages 282–86.

Tibetan words and names are rendered phonetically using a slightly adapted version of the phonetic transcription system featured on thlib .org. Sanskrit diacritics are used throughout the text.

Ga Rabjampa typically does not provide the names of the authors of the classical Indian treatises he cites, as these were well known to his original audience. These author names have occasionally been inserted into the present translation for the benefit of the modern reader.

ACKNOWLEDGMENTS

In this project, as in so many others, a debt of gratitude is owed to Sogyal Rinpoche, who offered constant support and encouragement to the translators. More than once, Alak Zenkar Rinpoche generously shared of his encyclopedic knowledge in order to shed light on the text's more arcane and elusive sections. For this and for so much else, we are honored and thankful.

Rigpa Translations' senior editor, Patrick Gaffney, was, as ever, a source of inspiration and guidance, and his expert reading of the translation led to many improvements in both style and substance.

Gyurme Avertin painstakingly read through the entire text, checking it against the original and spotting errors and omissions. Further proofreading was done by Angus Moore and Ani Ngawang Tsöndrü. Thanks are also due to Philip Philippou, Susie Godfrey, Stefan Eckel, Phillippa Sison, and Dominik Schloesser, as well as David Kittelstrom and all the staff at Wisdom for their assistance and support.

We also wish to acknowledge our indebtedness to previous translators of the *Seven Points of Mind Training*, particularly Chögyam Trungpa Rinpoche and Thupten Jinpa, whose brilliant and poetic renderings of the root verses are already imprinted in the minds and hearts of many English-speaking Dharma students, and rightly so.

Adam Pearcey
Rigpa Translations
Lerab Ling, France, May 2011

Introduction

❧⁂

The greatest obstacle to compassion and, in fact, to genuine happiness is our innate attitude of self-cherishing. According to the Buddhism of the Mahāyāna, or "Great Vehicle," constant preoccupation with our own interests and welfare, deriving from the mistaken belief in a concrete self-identity, is the source of all life's frustration and conflict. To remedy this and enable us to be of genuine service to others, we must meditate on loving kindness and compassion. Vividly bringing to mind the many forms of suffering that exist in the world, and even imagining our loved ones in difficult situations, we can gradually cultivate the sincere wish that all living beings may be freed entirely from any form of pain or misery and find lasting happiness. As we become more open, caring, and courageous, our own worries will steadily diminish. And as we continue along the path, compassion will deepen and extend ever further, until it encompasses even so-called enemies. At the same time, it will become increasingly effortless and spontaneous. Eventually, boundless compassion will simply radiate from us; all that we do—every word that we utter, every gesture that we make—will be of benefit to others.

This is the path of the bodhisattvas, and this is the training described in the present book, a pure spring of enlightened advice from the fifteenth century that retains its vitality even today.

THE TEXT

Ga Rabjampa's *Stream of Nectar: Pith Instructions for Cultivating Relative and Absolute Bodhicitta* is, as its name suggests, primarily concerned with the cultivation of *bodhicitta*, the "mind of enlightenment," in both its relative and absolute forms. While *relative bodhicitta*, according to its most popular definition, is the compassionate wish to attain perfect enlightenment for the sake of others, *absolute bodhicitta* refers to the direct realization of how things actually are, wisdom that is beyond subject-object duality. To arouse, maintain, and enhance these two types of bodhicitta is, in a sense, the essence of the entire Mahāyāna path, and so there are many techniques and approaches found in the various sources.

The text belongs to the broad category of *lojong*, or "mind training," primarily associated with the Kadam tradition founded by the Indian master Atiśa Dīpaṃkara Śrījñāna (982–1054) and his Tibetan disciple Dromtönpa Gyalwé Jungné (1004/5–64). More specifically, it is a commentary on the *Seven Points of Mind Training* attributed to Chekawa Yeshé Dorjé (1101–75). This collection of approximately seventy slogans,[1] arranged under seven headings by Chekawa's disciple Sechilpuwa Özer Zhönu (1121–89), inspired a great number of commentaries in Tibet,[2] many of which have now been translated into English.

Although Chekawa Yeshé Dorjé is often credited as the author of the *Seven Points*, it is clear that these teachings—including many of the actual slogans—predate him. In fact, Chekawa's most important contribution was to popularize what had until then been a closely guarded instruction, passed on to fortunate disciples in a "whispered lineage," by teaching it openly for the first time.

Unlike the gradual path (*lamrim*) teachings, which were also introduced into Tibet by Atiśa, the lojong teachings were intended only for students of the very highest capacity, which is why they were initially restricted. Of the three levels of capacity into which the gradual-path teachings categorize practitioners—lesser, middling, and greater—these instructions are intended only for those of the highest capacity, the followers of the bodhisattva path who seek complete and perfect enlightenment for the sake of all living beings. Yet even among the instructions belonging to this level, the approach followed here is considered a radical one.

Ga Rabjampa uses the example of straightening a crooked tree to explain how these teachings are more direct than others. Our habits of self-cherishing are so firmly rooted and deeply planted that a gradual approach will not work; we must pull strongly in the opposite direction, that of genuine altruism, by using the meditative practice of exchanging ourselves for others—"that most holy secret," as Śāntideva calls it. It is here that the uniqueness of these teachings—and this commentary in particular—becomes apparent.

References to the practice of exchanging oneself for others are to be found in the classical Indian texts, such as those of Nāgārjuna, Śāntideva, and Kamalaśīla—as Ga Rabjampa shows through his plentiful quotations. Yet what is only hinted at in those works is fully expressed here, especially in the detailed description of *tonglen*, the meditation practice of *giving*—or literally "sending"—our own happiness and well-being to others and *taking* upon ourselves their suffering. Even among Tibetan commentaries, Ga Rabjampa's account of this practice stands out as particularly vast and all-encompassing. The elaborate stages of visualization that he outlines incorporate elements more readily associated with practices such as *chö*—in which a purified, vastly expanded, and transformed version of the body is offered to various types of guests, including evil spirits—or *sang*—in which billowing clouds of fragrant juniper smoke transform into inexhaustible offerings of all that the different beings of the universe might desire, raining down upon them.

It would seem that Ga Rabjampa himself was aware of just how unusual his descriptions of the practice might appear, for he is keen to substantiate them through references to canonical sources. At the same time, he also cautions his readers not to be too narrow-minded like the well-dwelling frog in the famous story who explodes upon seeing the vastness of the ocean. These visualizations certainly do stretch the mind, he is telling us, but that is precisely the point—we need to take a radical approach if we are to overcome our inveterate habits of

self-cherishing and transform our attitude into one of boundless love
and compassion.

THE AUTHOR[3]

The author of our text, Ga Rabjampa Künga Yeshé, flourished during
what has been called a "golden age" for Tibetan Buddhism—a period
when many of Tibet's most celebrated scholars established what would
become the foundational tenets of their schools.[4] Longchen Rabjam,
Butön Rinchen Drup, the Third Karmapa Rangjung Dorjé, and Döl-
popa Sherap Gyaltsen all appeared in the century before Ga Rabjampa's
birth, and his own lifetime witnessed the careers of Jé Tsongkhapa and
his foremost disciples, including Gendün Drup, who would posthu-
mously receive the title of First Dalai Lama, as well as the Sakya master
Goram Sönam Sengé, who, like Ga Rabjampa himself, was a disciple
of both Rongtön Sheja Künrik and Ngorchen Künga Zangpo. This
same period saw the foundation of many new monasteries, such as the
"three great seats" of Ganden (1409), Drepung (1416), and Sera (1419),
the Sakya centers of Ngor (1430) and Nalendra (1436), as well as Tashi
Lhünpo (1447), future seat of the Panchen Lamas. In the coming years,
studies within these institutions would become increasingly formal-
ized, but for now the curriculums were not yet fixed, and monks fre-
quently traveled from one monastery or hermitage to another, often
studying with masters of different schools and lineages.

Ga Rabjampa Künga Yeshé was born in 1397 in the village of Dzonyak[5]
in Upper Ga in northwestern Kham, an area associated with the great
tenth-century Indian scholar Smṛtijñānakīrti. His father, Sangyé Kyap,
belonged to the ancient family of chieftains who ruled the area, and
his mother, Tarden Wangmo, possessed the signs and marks of a wisdom ḍākinī.[6] Before his birth, his mother dreamed of finding a statue of
the Buddha Maitreya, radiating brilliant light, in front of the Dzonyak
stūpa built by Smṛtijñānakīrti.

At six, Künga Yeshé entered the local monastery of Ga Nyidé, where
he learned to read and write with a lama called Changchup Zangpo.
Around this time, the lama gave extensive transmissions for the com-

plete works of the five Sakya patriarchs, attended by many local people, including the young Künga Yeshé. In spite of the long sessions, which left most people feeling tired and overcome by hunger and thirst, the young boy remained in perfect meditation posture throughout, causing the lama to remark, "Here is a bodhisattva whose potential has awakened. In the future he will be a great holder of the teachings." Some of those present even suggested he might be an incarnation of the great Smṛtijñānakīrti himself.

When he was eight years old, Künga Yeshé began his study of grammar and poetics and first received teachings on Smṛtijñānakīrti's *Weapon-Like Introduction to Speech*,[7] which inspired dreams indicating he was the master's incarnation. At the age of ten, he undertook a retreat on the deity Vajrabhairava according to the tradition of Ra Lotsāwa. One night the following year, he dreamed that he was about to be attacked by an elemental spirit (*jungpo*)[8] and immediately assumed the form of Vajrabhairava, beating sixteen *ḍamaru* drums in his sixteen right hands and ringing sixteen bells in his sixteen left hands, while uttering wrathful mantras and fiercely stomping his feet. His mother, asleep nearby, was disturbed by the noise and awoke to find her son standing, stomping his feet, and uttering the syllable *hūṃ*! In his vision, the spirit was expelled beyond the distant ocean, and from then on, it is said, no obstacles ever troubled him again.

At sixteen, he had a dream in which a lama appeared to him saying, "Son, do not remain here. Go to Ü-Tsang (Central Tibet). Follow teachers there and study and reflect. By becoming learned, you will benefit the teachings and beings. Do not tarry. Do not delay."

During the sixth month of that same year, he received novice ordination from Tekchen Chöjé Khenpo and Drung Chöjé Künga Rinchen. It was then that he received the name Künga Yeshé—Künga being the first name of both preceptors, and Yeshé (Skt. *jñāna*) to indicate that he was the incarnation of Smṛtijñānakīrti.

Shortly afterward, he journeyed to Central Tibet and first made his way to the great center of learning, Sangpu Neutok, where he met the great master Rongtön Shakya Gyaltsen (1367–1449). With Rongtön he then embarked upon an extraordinarily intensive period of study, receiving teachings on almost all the most important Indian treatises. During the breaks while Rongtön was away traveling and teaching, Künga Yeshé took the opportunity to study with some of the most learned masters of his day. With Nyetang Paṇchen Lodrö Tenpa Zhipa, he studied grammar, and while going through Smṛtijñānakīrti's *Weapon-Like Introduction to Speech*, he recalled the details of his past lives and had a vision in which he beheld Maitreya in golden form. From Martön Drepo Palden Rinchen at Chakla Drosa, he received teachings on the Abhidharma and Vinaya collections of the Buddhist scriptures. He also studied the Vinaya with Martön's nephew, Gyatso Rinchen, a teacher of the First Dalai Lama, Gendün Drup (1391–1474). At Sera Monastery, which had only recently been founded in 1419, he received teachings on Nāgārjuna's collection of reasoning and other Madhyamaka treatises from the great Gungru Gyaltsen Zangpo (1383–1450), the third throne-holder, who had studied with Jé Tsongkhapa in his youth. From Radrengpa Shakya Sönam (b. 1357?), a disciple of the great Ngülchu Tokmé Zangpo (1297–1371), he received a great many teachings on mind training, including the master's own composition entitled *The Flowing River of Bodhicitta*.

It was around this time that Künga Yeshé first met the great Ngorchen Künga Zangpo (1382–1457). Earlier, in Kham, he had been told by Drung Chöjé that at that time in the Sakya school there was none more learned in sūtra studies than Rongtön and none more learned in secret mantra[9] than Ngorchen, and so he should study with them both and master both disciplines. Thereafter, keeping this advice in his heart, he made sure to follow it. And so in 1417 he followed Ngorchen to Sakya, and after meeting the hierarchs, he went to see the great master at Shakzang Kumbum. He offered a maṇḍala, requesting empowerment and instructions, and before long was granted extensive teachings on the Path with Its Fruit (*lamdré*), as well as many other empowerments and transmissions.

In the iron-ox year of 1421, at the age of twenty-five, Künga Yeshé received full ordination in the great four-story temple of Sakya, with Künga Zangpo as preceptor, assisted by his younger brother, Zhönu Sengé. Zhönu Sengé became another of Künga Yeshé's main teachers, granting him empowerments, as well as teachings on the three sets of vows and on logic and epistemology. While at Sakya, Künga Yeshé also received teachings from Chöjé Zhönu Gyaltsen Chokpa,[10] including the master's own commentary on mind training and instructions on *Parting from the Four Attachments*. From the great scholar Pökhangpa Rinchen Gyaltsen (1348–1430), he received a detailed commentary on the three sets of vows as well as reading transmissions for the writings of Sazang Mati Paṇchen (1294–1376) and the six treatises of the Kadampas.[11]

On his way back to Sangpu, he visited the monastery of Zhalu, and when he saw an image of the great Butön Rinchen Drup (1290–1364), he realized that this was the master who had appeared to him in his dream, telling him to come to Central Tibet.

Once safely back at Sangpu, he continued his training with Rongtön, memorizing an incredible forty-two pages a day! In the spring of that year, he went on debating rounds at several monasteries, and on account of his prodigious learning, which gave him victory over everyone in debate, earned the title of Rabjampa.[12]

Finally, having accomplished all that he set out to achieve in Central Tibet, he returned to Kham. After spending more than a year with Drung Chöjé in Gatö, he renovated the practice cave at Dzonyak and entered retreat there in the water-hare year (1423) at the age of twenty-seven. For the next thirteen years, he put all his energy into practicing the teachings he had received in Central Tibet, especially Lamdré and the practice of Hevajra, moving from cave to cave and occasionally giving teachings and empowerments to disciples.

In the male fire-dragon year (1436), on the thirteenth day of the holy month of Saga Dawa, in a ceremony marked by auspicious signs, he founded the monastery of Śrī Tarlam Ganden Sazang Namgyal Ling. Shortly thereafter, in the newly opened monastery, he gave many transmissions, including that of the writings of the five Sakya patriarchs.

In the iron-horse year (1450) he learned that Rongtön, who had founded his great monastery of Nalendra in 1436, had recently passed away. Swiftly, he returned to Central Tibet in order to pay his respects before his former master's holy remains (*kudung*) at Nalendra. On the same trip, he also visited the famous Jowo statue in Lhasa and his former study college of Sangpu, where he made donations to all the monks.

Continuing on to Tsang, he visited the newly constructed monastery of Ngor (founded in 1430), presented offerings to his teacher Künga Zangpo, and received further instructions. In 1451 he visited Sakya, where he made a connection with the new hierarchs, including Dakchen Lodrö Wangchuk (b. 1402), and gave offerings to the monks. During his stay, he had a clear recollection of being at Sakya in his former lives and composed a praise of the monastery entitled *Ocean of Blessings*.

Once back at Tarlam, in the water-monkey year (1452), he gave extensive teachings on the *Seven Points of Mind Training*, accompanied by auspicious signs that included earth tremors, rainbows, a rain of white flowers, music heard from the sky, and the smell of incense pervading the air.[13]

In the earth-hare year (1459), aged sixty-three, he journeyed to Döndrup Ling Monastery,[14] where he met the Sakya hierarch, Dakchen Gyagarpa Sherap Gyaltsen (1436/39–95). Following their encounter, he was invited to teach at Döndrup Ling, and for the next few years spent his summers there and his winters at Tarlam. Much of his time during these later years of his life was spent in retreat.

Finally, in the year of the iron tiger (1470), at the beginning of the first month, he composed a prayer that included the lines: "As soon as the appearances of this life cease, may I be born in the heaven of Tuṣita, as the son of the protector Maitreya, and savor the glorious Mahāyāna teachings." Many times he told those around him that he would not remain for long. He asked his nephew Namgyal whether the index to the works of the five Sakya patriarchs had been completed, and on learning that it had not, told him to hurry. Some days later, when it was finished and offered to him, he expressed his delight. He later entrusted to his disciples his most sacred possession—an image of the *gandhola*[15] at Bodhgaya, handcrafted from nāga clay[16] by Smṛtijñānakīrti and containing many sacred relics.

Finally, as dawn broke on the morning of the thirteenth day of the second month, his heart-son Tsültrim Gyaltsen and his nephew Jamyang Künga offered him a padded cushion made of pure white cotton, requesting him to remain longer in the world. But he replied that his illness was too severe and that to stay would be of no benefit. Adopting the posture for the moment of death that is specified in the tantras, he exhaled and reabsorbed his mind into the mind of Maitreya. Thereafter, he remained in *tukdam*, a state of absorption in the luminous nature of mind, for three and a half days.

Ga Rabjampa's life, then, was typical of the age. Like his more famous contemporary Gorampa, he was born in Eastern Tibet but traveled to Central Tibet in order to study with some of the greatest masters of his day. After gaining the degree of Rabjampa, the highest qualification available, he returned to his homeland, where, after years of practice in retreat, he taught extensively and founded his own monastery, which, more than four hundred years later, would become the seat of Gatön Ngawang Lekpa, one of the key figures in the Nonsectarian (Rimé) movement, as well as of his principal disciple, Dezhung Rinpoche.

His Writings

Ga Rabjampa left behind four volumes of writing, which include:
- A commentary on the *Hevajra Tantra*
- A commentary on *Chanting the Names of Mañjuśrī*
- A commentary on the *Sarvadurgatipariśodhana Tantra*
- A commentary on the *Seven Points of Mind Training* (translated in this volume)
- An overview of Maitreya's *Ornament of Clear Realization*
- A commentary on the detailed explanation of the branches of the *Ornament of Clear Realization*
- Writings on the three turnings of the wheel of Dharma, the twentyfold saṅgha, dependent origination, and the dhyānas and formless absorptions
- An overview of Maitreya's *Ornament of Mahāyāna Sūtras*
- A commentary on Maitreya's *Sublime Continuum*
- An overview of the Vinaya
- A commentary on Guṇaprabha's *Vinaya Sūtra*
- An overview of Vasubandhu's *Treasury of Abhidharma*

- A summary of logic and epistemology (*pramāṇa*)
- A maṇḍala rite for *Guhyasamāja Mañjuvajra*
- A clarification of difficult points in the *Hevajrābhisamayaṭīkā*
- An explanation of the body maṇḍala
- A praise of the masters of Sakya Monastery called *Ocean of Blessings*
- A praise of the Anyen Dampa "uncle and nephew"[17] called *Beautiful Rosary of Jewels*
- A praise of Drung Tsültrim Gyaltsen[18] called *Rosary of Jewels*
- Other praises
- A fulfillment and healing rite called *Eliminating All Obstacles*
- Songs of realization
- An aspiration prayer called *The Heart of the Mahāyāna Path*
- An aspiration prayer for mind training called *The Excellent Path to Enlightenment* (translated in the appendix of the present volume)
- Plus a large record of teachings received (*gsan yig*) in 133 folios.

Several reasons have been put forward to account for the enduring popularity of the lojong teachings, and especially the *Seven Points*. Suggestions include the accessibility of the slogans, the astute psychological insights they convey, and the transformative power they hold. All are undoubtedly true. Clear and concise, these sayings can serve as poignant reminders and guidelines for all who aspire to follow in the footsteps of the great Kadampa geshés of old or even of the bodhisattvas who transcend ordinary space and time.

As Sogyal Rinpoche said (of the Dzogchen teachings, although it applies equally here):

> I have also found that modern people want a path shorn of dogma, fundamentalism, exclusivity, complex metaphysics, and culturally exotic paraphernalia, a path at once simple and profound, a path that does not need to be practiced in ashrams or monasteries but one that can be integrated with ordinary life and practiced anywhere.[19]

The lojong teachings presented here are simple and profound, and they can be integrated with ordinary life in the modern world. It is our hope that even in a text such as this, written more than five hundred years ago in a remote part of eastern Tibet, universal relevance and ageless wisdom may be easily discerned.

Seven Points of Mind Training

---

1. The Preliminaries
First, train in the preliminaries.

2. The Main Practice
Once stability is reached, teach the secret.
Train in the two—giving and taking—alternately.
These two are to be mounted on the breath.
Begin the process of taking with yourself.
The instruction for periods between meditation is, in brief:
three objects, three poisons, and three roots of virtue.
In all activities, train by applying slogans.
Consider all things and events as dreamlike.
Examine the nature of unborn awareness.
Let even the antidote be freed in its own place.
Rest in the ālaya, the essence of the path.
The seven and their processes are conceptual, so forsake them.
Between sessions, be a conjurer of illusions.

3. Transforming Adversity
When all the world is overrun[20] with evil,
transform adversity into the path of enlightenment.
Drive all blames into one.
Meditate on the great kindness of all.
Meditating on delusory perceptions as the four kāyas

is the unsurpassable protection of emptiness.
The fourfold practice is the best of methods.
Whatever you encounter, apply the practice.
When the two are complete, take on all.
Transform the unfavorable into supports for meditation.
First address whatever is most prominent.

4. Applying the Practice throughout the Whole of Life
The essence of the instruction, briefly stated,
is to apply yourself to the five strengths.
The Mahāyāna advice for transference
involves the same five strengths. Conduct is important.[21]

5. The Measure of Mind Training
The measure of the training is in turning away.
A sign of proficiency is to have five greatnesses.
All teachings share a single objective.[22]
Of the two witnesses, rely upon the principal one.
Always maintain only a joyful attitude.
If this can be done even when distracted, you are proficient.

6. The Commitments of Mind Training
Train constantly in three basic principles.
Change your attitude, but remain natural.
Don't speak of injured limbs.
Don't ponder others' flaws.
Train first with the strongest destructive emotions.
Abandon any expectations of results.
Give up poisonous food.
Don't be so loyal to the cause.
Don't lash out in retaliation.
Don't lie in ambush.
Don't strike a vulnerable point.
Don't transfer the ox's burden to the cow.[23]

Don't be competitive.
Don't misperform the rites.
Don't reduce gods to demons.
Don't seek others' misery as crutches of your own happiness.

7. The Precepts of Mind Training
Do everything with a single intention.
Counter all adversity with a single remedy.
Two tasks: one at the beginning and one at the end.
Whichever of the two occurs, be patient.
Keep the two, even at your life's expense.
Train in the three difficulties.
Acquire the three main provisions.
Cultivate the three that must not decline.
Keep the three from which you must not separate.
Apply the training impartially to all.
It is vital that it be deep and all-pervasive.
Meditate constantly on those who've been set apart.[24]
Don't be dependent on external conditions.
This time, practice what's most important.
Don't misunderstand.
Don't be inconsistent.
Train wholeheartedly.
Gain freedom through discernment and analysis.
Don't be boastful.[25]
Don't be irritable.
Don't be temperamental.
Don't seek acknowledgment.

This essence of the nectar-like instructions
for transforming into the path of awakening
the five prevalent signs of degeneration
was passed down from the one from Golden Isle.
When karmic seeds left over from former trainings

were aroused in me, I felt great interest, and so,
without regard for suffering or disparagement,
I sought instructions on subduing ego-clinging.
Now, even in death, I will have no regrets.

The Stream of Nectar

*Pith Instructions for Cultivating Relative
and Absolute Bodhicitta*

Ga Rabjampa Künga Yeshé

*Respectfully, I pay homage to the noble masters and most exalted
    of deities!*

*To that which dispels entirely the darkness of our faults,
source of every virtue, goodness, and precious quality,
the ground sustaining the whole infinity of beings—
to the precious mind of bodhicitta, I pay homage!*

*Inconceivable, a manifestation of wisdom and love,
you work for those worn down and lacking all protection,
liberating them from the vast ocean of existence and quiescence—
to you, most compassionate and supreme guides, I pay homage!*

*Always considering the benefit of beings,
having realized the wondrous twofold bodhicitta,
you shed your brilliant light upon the Supreme Vehicle's noble path—
great bodhisattvas, grant me your protection!*

*Herein I shall now explain this flowing stream of nectar,
    a pith instruction
for meditating on bodhicitta, bestower of supreme immortality,
a wish-granting tree to fulfill the hopes of living beings,
and faultless pathway to the citadel of omniscience.*

*All who seek to benefit beings for as long as space exists,
by first crossing the ocean of unsurpassable qualities,
with the fully developed wings of the profound and vast—
all you fortunate ones, take joy in this and listen well!*

Here, the topic to be explained is the pith instruction on mind training according to the Great Vehicle. This is the single path that is followed by all the buddhas of the three times and their heirs, the essence of the teachings of the Great Vehicle, the ultimate of all pith instructions, the most profound instruction of the oral lineage and the quintessence of the ocean of all the excellent teachings.

The completely and perfectly enlightened buddhas, with a view to the different capacities of beings to be guided, teach various systems of training, but all of them, whether directly or indirectly, lead to the ultimate cause, which is the path of the Great Vehicle, and the ultimate fruition, which is omniscience. As it says in the *Chapter of the Truthful One*:

> Mañjuśrī, all the teachings I have given to sentient beings are for the sake of attaining omniscient wisdom. They all lead to awakening. They all arrive at the Great Vehicle and the attainment of omniscient wisdom. Since they all lead to the same destination, I have not set forth a variety of different vehicles.

The reason for this is as follows. It is only in complete and perfect buddhahood that all faults without exception are eliminated and all qualities without exception are fully developed, and the attainment of this can come only through the profound and vast path of the Great Vehicle.

As it says in Maitreya's *Ornament of Mahāyāna Sūtras* (1:7):

> Because it is profound and because it is vast,
> it ripens fully and is beyond the conceptual.
> Therefore, it teaches with two aspects
> and is the method of the unsurpassed.

It is reasonable, therefore, for individuals with inquiring minds—those who have reflected on the potential benefits and losses to be incurred in future existences and who wish to secure their own and others' benefit and happiness—to exert themselves on the path of the Great Vehicle, without undue concern for their present lives or physical well-being. Moreover, since the most important factors on this path are relative bodhicitta, which is rooted in great compassion, and absolute bodhicitta, which is the wisdom that transcends the two extremes, we can be sure that these constitute the basic cause for the attainment of perfect enlightenment. With this point in mind, the sublime Lord of Nāgas (i.e., Nāgārjuna) said [in the *Precious Garland* 2:74–75]:

> If we ourselves and all the world
> wish for unsurpassed enlightenment,
> its basis is bodhicitta
> stable as the king of mountains,
> compassion reaching out in all directions,
> and wisdom that transcends duality.

This explanation of the pith instructions for meditating on precious bodhicitta is divided into two parts: (1) the successive stages of the incomparable lineage, and (2) the method for putting the instructions into practice.

1. The Lineage of Practice

⚜

The great and glorious bodhisattva Atiśa Dīpaṃkara, who was truly a second Buddha in this degenerate age, a beacon shedding the light of the teachings upon the world, and a guide for the Tibetan people, possessed unimaginable instructions on training in bodhicitta, but among them, three streams of transmission are most important.[26]

The *first* of these he received from his teacher, the mendicant Dharmarakṣita, who actually offered his own flesh to heal a sick person and was graced with a vision of Ārya Avalokiteśvara. This is the tradition of cultivating the bodhicitta of equalizing self and others in the beginning.

The *second* he received from his teacher, Maitrīyogi, also known as Kusali the Younger, who through meditating exclusively on love and compassion saw the Buddha Maitreya face to face, so that he became known as Maitrīyogi, the "yogin of Maitreya." Although this teacher also held the instructions of the third transmission and therefore appears in that lineage as well, he was mainly a holder of the teachings from Ārya Mañjuśrī, the instructions of Nāgārjuna as passed down through Śāntideva. This is the tradition of cultivating bodhicitta once the equalizing of self and others has been accomplished.

The *third* transmission was that of the heart practice and extraordinary pith instructions of the great scholar Dharmakīrti of Suvarṇadvīpa (Tib. Serlingpa). This is the tradition of meditating on exchanging oneself for others from the very beginning.

The extended lineage of this instruction is as follows.

Our teacher, the king of the Śākyas, during his life as the great brahman Samudrarenu, was overwhelmed by exceptionally great compassion, and as a result he made five hundred aspirations, including one to help the beings of a future age rife with the five degenerations, whose merit would be weak and who would be difficult to tame, by revealing to them a convenient path involving very little hardship. Through the force of these aspirations, he appeared during this age of conflict, manifested the attainment of enlightenment in this world of Patient Endurance,[27] and turned the inconceivable wheel of Dharma. The essence of these teachings, contained in this nectar-like instruction, he transmitted to the holy regent Maitreya, who during his previous life as the monk called Sthiramati had meditated solely on loving kindness and attained realization. Through the power of this meditation, when he was on one occasion setting foot on the threshold of a great city, he prayed, "May the minds of all who live in this land be filled with loving kindness!" As a result, in place of his ordination name, he became known simply as Maitreya, the "Loving One." From that moment until his awakening, he will continue to be known by this name.

In turn, Ārya Asaṅga, who traveled to the heaven of Tuṣita, received from him inconceivable transmissions and instructions on the Mahāyāna sūtras, including the Five Treatises of Maitreya, and gained the realization of the third bodhisattva level. The *Mañjuśrī Root Tantra* states:

> There will appear a monk by the name of Asaṅga
> who is learned in the treatises
> and will make many clear distinctions
> between the sūtras' definitive and provisional meanings.

And it is also said:

> So that the teachings may remain long into the future,
> he will compile the actual meaning of the sūtras.
> He will live for a hundred and fifty years,
> and, having left his body, will depart for the heavens.
> While circling through the realms of existence,

he will enjoy the taste of lasting happiness,
and ultimately this great being
will attain awakening.

It was to this great pioneering master, prophesied in many such statements from the sūtras and tantras, that Maitreya transmitted the teachings.

Asaṅga, in turn, passed the teachings on to his own younger brother, the all-knowing Vasubandhu, who for five hundred lifetimes without interruption had been born as a pandit skilled in the five sciences. Vasubandhu had gained indomitable confidence through his learning. He recited aloud many thousands of texts[28] and composed several commentaries at the command of Ārya Maitreya, becoming renowned throughout this world of Jambudvīpa[29] as the second omniscient one.

Vasubandhu had four great disciples who were more learned than himself in certain topics. Of these, it was to Ārya Vimuktisena, more learned than his master in the subject of the Perfection of Wisdom, that Vasubandhu passed on these instructions. Vimuktisena, who was the nephew of the great Buddhadasa, reached the bodhisattva level of Perfect Joy[30] and, having received instructions on the Perfection of Wisdom directly from the Buddha, composed his great commentary.[31]

In turn, Ārya Vimuktisena passed these instructions to the great scholar Bhadanta Vimuktisena, who was on the Mahāyāna path of accumulation, the so-called "stage of devotion," and composed several treatises including a commentary on the *Perfection of Wisdom in 25,000 Lines*.

Bhadanta Vimuktisena passed these instructions down to the master Guṇamitra, who was a teacher of Haribhadra and a student of the greatly accomplished Buddhajñāna, and who requested the composition of the commentary on the *Verse Summary of the Perfection of Wisdom*.

In turn, Guṇamitra passed these instructions to Haribhadra, who, having received authority from Buddha Maitreya, composed many treatises including a commentary on the eight-thousand-line text[32] and worked for the sake of the teachings of the Perfection of Wisdom.

Haribhadra, in turn, passed these instructions to the master Pūrṇa-vadhana, who was a great pandit and the author of several treatises including a commentary to Vasubandhu's *Treasury of Abhidharma*.

Pūrṇavadhana passed these instructions to Kusali the Elder, who spent all his time practicing in isolated retreat and became known as a great adept of the two kinds of bodhicitta.

Kusali the Elder passed these teachings to Kusali the Younger, who was able to take the sufferings of others directly upon himself.

Kusali the Younger transmitted these instructions to Serlingpa.

As regards the shorter lineage of transmission, Serlingpa is said to have received the teachings directly from the Buddha Maitreya. Son of a king of the Golden Isle (Suvarṇadvīpa),[33] Serlingpa possessed many exceptional qualities. It was said, for example, that at the very moment of his birth, he took refuge in the Three Jewels. On account of his great scholarship, his reputation spread throughout the whole of Jambud-vīpa, and he worked extensively for the sake of the teachings, by lead-ing all the non-Buddhists in his country to the Buddhadharma and in many other ways. He was a perfect embodiment of bodhicitta.

Serlingpa passed this transmission on to the glorious Lord Atiśa, whose fame extends throughout the three worlds. The details of Atiśa's life can be learned from the extensive biographies, but here is a brief summary.

He was born as the son of Kalyanaśrī, the king of Zahor, and imme-diately upon his birth he had a vision of Ārya Tārā. From an early age he studied the five sciences, especially the four classes of tantra, so that he became supremely learned. His learned and accomplished teachers, whom he followed and served genuinely and authentically, included Śāntipa, Serlingpa, and Vidyākokila. From the moment he first received the Hevajra empowerment from his guru Rāhulagupta, he had visions of many yidam deities.[34] He mastered inconceivable forms of samādhi meditation. In accordance with prophecies he received from several masters and yidam deities, directly and in dreams, he took ordination within the Mahāsaṅghika tradition. He gained clairvoyance and mirac-ulous abilities and subjugated demons and *tīrthika* philosophers.[35] He received instructions on mind training from the gurus mentioned above and from his yidam deities, and twofold bodhicitta flooded his mind, expanding like a river in summertime.

In particular, when he realized that the great master of Suvarṇadvīpa was a perfect embodiment of the bodhicitta teachings, he traveled to the Golden Isle to seek instruction. As soon as the two masters met, Atiśa recognized Serlingpa as his teacher from former lives and felt boundless devotion. The guru offered him a golden statue [of the Buddha] that he had found in the forest as a child, symbolically empowering him as the holder of his teachings. Atiśa spent a total of twelve years receiving instructions, all the while staying close to his guru,[36] and the bodhicitta of cherishing others above himself was born within his mind.

Once he returned to India, he became an elder at Vikramaśīla Monastery, from where his enlightened activity spread in all directions, east and west. He was revered as a master by followers of all schools without exception, and he caused the teachings of sūtra and mantra to spread far and wide both through teaching and through practice. His yidam deities, including Tārā and Khasarpaṇi,[37] and many of his teachers, such as Rāhula, told him of the benefit that would come from traveling to Tibet, especially how it would benefit a certain lay practitioner[38] and cause the teachings of his oral lineage to flourish. Atiśa also received several invitations from the nephew of Lha Lama Yeshé Ö [i.e., Jangchup Ö], who had himself been prophesied by the Buddha.

So it was that he went to Tibet, where he took pity on the ignorant Tibetans and cleared away their mistaken views and practices through scriptural authority and logical reasoning and set them upon the genuine path. He set ablaze the torch of the sacred Dharma, burning away the thickets of mistaken views, caused the eye of intelligence to develop in people's minds so that they could see the nature of reality, and showed clearly the distinction between Dharma and non-Dharma. In the fertile minds of fortunate disciples, he planted the seeds of bodhicitta and watered them with the finest nectar-like explanations, so that they ripened into a wondrous harvest of liberation. And the mansion-like intellect of his foremost heir, the great Dromtönpa, in particular, he filled with jewels of transmission and realization. As if opening up the treasure chest of his precious oral lineage, he dispelled the spiritual poverty of the Land of Snows, bringing bountiful riches of virtue and goodness. We should appreciate, therefore, that the glorious Atiśa, holder of this precious oral lineage, which is like a chain of golden mountains, was even kinder to Tibetans than the Buddha himself.

Dromtönpa Gyalwé Jungné was a vital upholder of the teachings. He was blessed with visions of several yidam deities, including Ārya Tārā, and received indications that in his next life he would go to Tuṣita, into the presence of his teacher, Jowo Atiśa. It was to this master, then, who was like the single eye of the Tibetan people, that Atiśa transmitted all the general teachings of the sūtras, tantras, and pith instructions, as if filling a vase to the brim. This instruction Atiśa transmitted to him in secret, for it was like giving away a most highly treasured jewel kept deep inside his heart.

Dromtönpa gave these teachings to a few suitable disciples, including his foremost spiritual heirs known as the "three precious brothers." In particular, he transmitted them to the great Potowa Rinchen Salwa, that victory banner of the teachings who was renowned as an emanation of the great elder Aṅgiraja, and who worked exclusively for the sake of the Dharma, in both study and practice, and lived together with more than two thousand monks who had abandoned any concern for the present life. Not even for a single instant did this great master indulge in the eight worldly concerns in either thought or deed, and besides the immediate need to deal with comings and goings whenever they arose, he entertained no grand projects nor any speculation about the future.

Potowa had eight great spiritual heirs, but among them all it was to the pair renowned as the "sun and moon of Central Tibet"—Sharawa Yönten Drak, who possessed the vast vision of Dharma, and the great Langtangpa Dorjé Sengé, who had mastery over bodhicitta—that he transmitted these teachings in secret, having first extracted the main points and condensed them into pith instructions.

The great Sharawa had visions in which he saw many yidam deities face to face. The light of his wisdom expanded through the study of an unimaginably vast number of Dharma teachings, and his natural intelligence was unparalleled. It was from him that the precious master Chekawa Yeshé Dorjé received the transmission.

Chekawa Yeshé Dorjé was born into a Nyingmapa family and trained his mind according to the teachings of many sutras and tantras. From an early age, he took the sufferings of others upon himself and felt natural joy in doing so. His potential and capacity for the Mahāyāna were greatly developed. At the age of twenty-six, in Yarlung, he heard the *Eight Verses* of Langri Thangpa from Geshé Nyangchak Shingpa, and this caused him to feel great devotion to the Kadam teachings. Confident that the bodhicitta of exchanging oneself for others must be the fundamental basis of the Mahāyāna teachings, he spent four years studying with Potowa's disciples Geshé Dölpa and Luk Mepa and received all manner of instructions on the texts of the Kadam tradition.

Having developed deep confidence in bodhicitta, he went to Uri at the age of thirty to seek instructions on mind training. For two years he received teachings from the great Sharawa, but during this time he never heard even a casual reference to the instructions he sought. Feeling somewhat doubtful, he asked his teacher, "Is the exchanging of oneself and others not the root of the Dharma?" Sharawa replied, "Indeed, it is indispensable as a method for attaining awakening," and he made this clear with a quotation from [Nāgārjuna's] *Precious Garland*. Gaining in confidence, Chekawa requested the instructions. Sharawa accepted and Chekawa studied with him for a further nine years—six years at first and another three later on—focusing entirely on this practice. He meditated upon whatever teachings he received, so that he cut through the bonds of self-cherishing, and bodhicitta was truly born within him.

Chekawa knew mind training to be the essence of the Dharma, but he thought few would be capable of receiving it, so initially he was reluctant to teach it. Then, out of compassion, he taught some lepers who had been forsaken by the doctors and had abandoned any hope of finding happiness in life. As a result of the practice, they were cured of their leprosy and gained great realization. Before long, many more patients came to him, and the instructions soon became known as "Chekawa's leprosy Dharma." In time, he saw that the teaching could benefit others on a vast scale, and he began to impart them more widely, teaching vast assemblies. So it was that he became a great master of these instructions and an incomparable bodhisattva.

It was from Chekawa that the great Sechilpuwa Özer Zhönu received these teachings and brought them all together, spending twenty-four years in Chengyi Lhading and other places, meditating on whatever he received. As a result, just as in the slogan, "You are well trained if you can practice even while distracted," even in the face of major difficulties, by applying the antidotes, he was able to transform adversities and take them as part of the path. Gaining many other unimaginable qualities too as signs of progress, he taught these instructions widely, to large gatherings, as well as transmitting them in secret, according to the situation. Through taking these teachings as the heart of his own practice, he became a great bodhisattva.

Sechilpuwa gave the teachings to the Lord of Lhalung, Özer Lama, who in turn gave them to Lhadingpa Jangchup Bum, who passed them on to Lhading Ön.[39] He gave them to the diligent practitioner and abbot Dampa Yönten Pal, who gave them to the great abbot Dewa Pal, who gave them to the learned and disciplined Kazhipa Drakpa Zhönu.[40]

He, in turn, gave them to Sönam Drakpa, who possessed inconceivable qualities of learning and realization, and was the most precious and sacred crown jewel of all the holders of the teaching.

Sönam Drakpa gave them to the emanation of Ārya Avalokiteśvara, Gyalsé Tokmé Zangpo, who is as famous as the sun and moon, and who possessed unimaginable good qualities in great abundance, so much so that fortunate disciples with purity of vision perceived him directly as Avalokiteśvara, the Lord of the World. In fact, it was by means of these very instructions that this great bodhisattva became just like a second Buddha.

He, in turn, passed these instructions to the great bodhisattva known as Yeshé Pal.[41] This master, having seen the nature of dependent origination, just as it is, beyond conceptual elaboration, destroyed any conceptual focus involving grasping at characteristics, and from the clouds of his nonreferential compassion, there poured down rains of pure enlightened activity, which ripened the crops of virtue in his disciples. In this, he was a precious and incomparable lord of Dharma, entirely without equal in this world.

In the presence of this great master, through his inexpressible kindness, I received transmissions of texts, reasoning, and pith instructions in general, and this very teaching in particular, many times in the style known as "guidance according to experience" (*nyams khrid*).

There are several other ways in which this transmission has come down to us, including the lineage passing from the omniscient Vasubandhu to Sthiramati and the rest, that from the great Chengawa to Shawo Gangpa and the rest, that from the lord of Lhalung to Lha Drowa Gönpo and the rest, and that from Gyalsé Tokmé to Gyamawa Yönten Ö.

For my part, I also received this essence of the teachings many times as a result of my exceedingly great devotion and interest, firstly from the bodhisattva Samten Rinchenpa, then from the great bodhisattva and Lord of Dharma Radrengpa Shakya Sönam, and from the great renunciate of Drosa, Özer Künga Pal, and finally from the great Vajradhara of this degenerate age, [Ngorchen] Künga Zangpo; but fearing that it might take too much space, I will not describe these other lineages in detail.

⁓❦⁓

Abiding at the center of the vast ocean of teachings,
you rule over the jewel island of transmission and realization
and bring down a rain of nectar-like immaculate instructions—
powerful nāga-like lords of the oral lineage, in you I put my faith!

2. Following a Spiritual Teacher

———— ✧ ————

I will now show how the instructions that have been passed down through this lineage are put into practice.

According to the great whispered lineage they are divided into preparation, main part, and conclusion, whereas according to the *Seven Points*, they are divided into:
1. Preliminaries, the basis for practice
2. Main part, training in twofold bodhicitta
3. Transforming adversity into the path of awakening
4. Applying the practice throughout our lives
5. The measure of mind training
6. Commitments of mind training
7. Precepts for mind training

In the vajra verses of the whispered lineage, it says:

First, train in the preliminaries.

When the meaning of this is put into practice, there are the following five themes to focus on:
1. Guru yoga, as a means of swiftly receiving blessings
2. Reflecting on the difficulty of finding the freedoms and advantages, as a means of developing the intention to make this life meaningful
3. Reflecting on death and impermanence, as a means of swiftly spurring yourself on to diligence

4. Reflecting on the cause and effect of actions, as a means of properly adopting or avoiding a course of action
5. Reflecting on the trials of saṃsāra, as a means of developing a special attitude of renunciation

GURU YOGA, THE METHOD FOR SWIFTLY RECEIVING BLESSINGS

Although the practice of guru yoga is not to be found in the sūtra approach, following a spiritual teacher is taught as the root of the path in all the higher and lower vehicles. As it says in Nāgārjuna's *Letter to a Friend* (verse 62):

> To follow a spiritual friend is to perfect entirely
> the purest form of conduct, said the Buddha.
> So follow noble beings, for there are many indeed
> who relied upon the buddhas and gained peace.

Following a teacher correctly is taught to be an utterly pure form of conduct. Its benefits are evident from history.

Well then, you might think, what kind of teacher should we follow? Maitreya's *Ornament of Mahāyāna Sūtras* (17:10) says:

> Follow a spiritual teacher who is disciplined, peaceful, utterly serene,
> endowed with special qualities, diligent, rich in scriptural learning,
> highly realized concerning the nature of reality, skilled in speaking,
> the embodiment of love, and indefatigable.

This outlines ten qualifications. The meaning is as follows:
1. Through the higher training in discipline, his faculties will be *disciplined*.
2. Through the higher training in meditation, his mind will remain *peaceful*.

3. Through the higher training in wisdom, his destructive emotions will be *utterly pacified*.
4. He will possess greater *qualities* than his students.
5. He will be *diligent* and enthusiastic in benefiting others.
6. He will be *rich in knowledge* of the three collections of scriptures.
7. He will possess the wisdom of *realizing* the natural state of reality.
8. He will be *skilled in communicating* the Dharma to others.
9. His motivation will be pure, since he is *loving* and has no concern for respect or material possessions.
10. He will be *indefatigable*, never tired by the hardships involved in teaching Dharma.

In a similar vein, Śāntideva's *Introduction to the Bodhisattva's Way of Life* (5:102) says:

> Never, even at the cost of my life,
> will I forsake my spiritual teacher,
> who is learned in the Mahāyāna
> and supreme in bodhisattva discipline.

As this says, we must follow a noble spiritual teacher who is learned in the meaning of the Mahāyāna teachings and who upholds the discipline of the bodhisattvas, cherishing him as dearer than even our own life. The same text (5:103) describes how to follow the teacher:

> I must train in following my teacher,
> as described in the life of Śrī Sambhava.

When the boy Śrī Sambhava and the girl Śrīmati taught the bodhisattva's discipline to Sudhana at the gateway to the city of Sumanamukha, they explained, in elaborate detail and with clear logic, how to follow a spiritual teacher. They said:

> Son of good family, spiritual teachers are like mothers, giving birth to the family of buddhas; they are like fathers,

accomplishing vast benefit; they are like nurses, protecting us from all harmful deeds; they are like mentors, leading us to understand the bodhisattva training; they are like guides, leading us along the path of the perfections; they are like doctors, curing the disease of the destructive emotions; they are like snow-capped mountains, nurturing the herbs of wisdom; they are like brave warriors, protecting us from all fear; they are like ferrymen, carrying us across the great river of saṃsāra;[42] spiritual teachers are like oarsmen, rowing us to the jewel isle of omniscient wisdom.

Therefore, son of good family, constantly keeping these ideas in mind, you must honor your spiritual teacher. With a mind like the earth, bear all burdens without ever tiring; like a diamond, your will unbreakable; like a mountain range, unperturbed by any suffering; like a servant, doing whatever is required; like an apprentice, never disobeying an instruction; like a common slave, never refusing to carry out a task; like a nurse, not upset by destructive emotions; like a sweeper, abandoning pride; like a vehicle, carrying any load; like a mountain, unmoving; like a dog, not growing angry; like a bull with broken horns, free from all arrogance; with your attitude like that of a bright child, looking up at the face of the spiritual teacher. You must honor the spiritual teacher with your mind like that of a youthful prince, acting without transgressing the commands of the Dharma-king.

Son of good family, consider yourself to be someone who is sick; your spiritual teacher, a doctor; his instructions, medicine; and diligent practice, the healing process.

Consider yourself a traveler; your spiritual teacher, a guide; his instructions, the path; and diligent practice, safe passage.

Consider yourself a passenger crossing to the far shore; your spiritual teacher, a ferryman; his teachings, a dock; and diligent practice, a boat.

Consider yourself a farmer; your spiritual teacher, a lord of nāgas; his teachings, rain; and diligent practice, the harvest.

Consider yourself impoverished; your spiritual teacher, a benefactor; his instructions, wealth; and diligent practice, overcoming poverty.

Consider yourself an apprentice; your spiritual teacher, a mentor; his instructions, the craft; and diligent practice, gaining mastery.

Consider yourself beset with fear; your spiritual teacher, a brave warrior; his instructions, weapons; and diligent practice, vanquishing all foes.

Consider yourself a merchant; your spiritual teacher, the captain of a ship; his instructions, treasure; and diligent practice, the taking of the bounty.

Consider yourself a good son; your spiritual teacher, a parent; his instructions, the family trade; and diligent practice, its perpetuation.

Son of good family, consider yourself a prince; your spiritual teacher, the Dharma king and his ministers; his instructions, the laws of the realm; and diligent practice, donning the royal crown, complete with ornaments and insignia, to oversee the citadel of a sovereign of the Dharma.

After this, the benefits of following a spiritual teacher are taught in detail. In summary, the text [of the *Gaṇḍavyūha Sūtra*] says:

Son of good family, in short, it is like this. All the actions of the bodhisattvas, all the transcendent perfections, levels, doors of meditative concentration (*samādhi*), attainment of the wisdom of higher perceptions, powers of unfailing memory, fearless eloquence, wisdom of dedication, boundless qualities, fulfillment of the bodhisattvas' aspirations, and the attainment and perfection of all the qualities of buddhahood—all depends on the spiritual teacher.

The text continues by saying that spiritual teachers are the *source* of these qualities, that the qualities *arise from them*, and that spiritual teachers are their *cause*.

We must understand this, just as it is stated here so clearly, and then put it into practice.

In summary, as it says in the *Ornament* [*of Mahāyāna Sūtras*] (ch. 18):

> Follow the spiritual teacher by showing respect,
> by offering gifts, by service, and by practice.

We follow the spiritual teacher by showing respect—through offering prostrations and so on; by offering gifts, such as Dharma robes; by serving him, washing his feet, and so on; and by practice, through taking his instructions to heart. Of these, the last is the most important.

The method for following a spiritual teacher that is taught in the texts of the Vajrayāna is, as it says in the Aśvaghoṣa's *Fifty Stanzas on Following a Teacher*, "the root of all paths, the source of all accomplishments, the entrance to all blessings, and the most important of all practices."

What we call *guru yoga* is a method for becoming accustomed to following the teacher in this way, by using the skillful techniques of visualization, and as such it is an extraordinary feature of the secret mantra vehicle. Nevertheless, among the earlier masters of these pith instructions, some would bring their practice within the fold of the Mantra Vehicle and perform this meditation as a preliminary to the session.

The way to do so is as follows.

In an inspiring place, far from the hustle and bustle of ordinary activity, seat yourself comfortably, either with your legs crossed or simply in an upright position. Let go of all the ordinary thoughts whirling in your mind—thoughts of overcoming rivals, helping friends, or amassing wealth. As a preliminary, meditate on taking refuge, arousing bodhicitta, cultivating the immeasurables, and so on. Then visualize your root teacher, in the form of Avalokiteśvara, above your head in the space before you. Decide, with complete conviction, that he is the embodiment of all the gurus, yidam deities, buddhas, all the sacred Dharma, and all the saṅgha. Consider that, together with all others, you emanate bodies as numerous as atoms in the universe, and perform practices for accumulating merit and purifying obscurations, before merging your mind with his.

More specifically, offer gifts that you have actually arranged, as well as those created in your imagination, including your own body, possessions, and sources of merit. Extending the scope of your visualization, offer the seven-point maṇḍala,[43] counting as you do so, a hundred times or more. Pray with strong faith and devotion, and trust that the teacher's blessings have been invoked and you are infused with the blessings of his enlightened body, speech, and mind. Form a resolute wish that your obscurations may be purified, and then consider that the teacher dissolves into you, and so on, in the usual way.

In particular here, at the stage of prayer, pray that you may receive the teacher's blessings so that love, compassion, and bodhicitta arise in your mind. Pray too that adversity may be transformed into the path of awakening and so on. Like this, pray ardently for the fulfillment of your wishes.

After the session, during all your actions, bring to mind the kindness of the teacher. Avoid ordinary patterns of thought and focus instead on enlightened qualities. Train in developing unshakable faith. Without the slightest pretense or deception, serve and gratify the teacher, aspiring that you may never part company. And dedicate all the sources of your merit toward awakening.

In short, know that of all the prayers that could be made in the teacher's presence, the most important is for the two kinds of bodhicitta to arise in the mind, to remain and to increase further and further. At all times and in all situations, do not allow your mind to be without fervent faith and devotion. Think only of the teacher. To arouse such mindfulness recite verses like the following, and reflect upon their meaning:

> The sun's rays are imbued with tremendous heat
> yet, without a magnifying glass, can produce no flame.
> Likewise, the buddhas transmit their blessings,
> but without the teacher, they'll not be received.

꤫

Dispeller of all ills, source of everything desirable in saṃsāra and nirvāṇa,
you are the supreme and all-powerful sovereign, my genuine teacher,
to follow you devotedly, like Sadāprarudita and the youthful Sudhana,
is indeed the most excellent of good fortune.

3. The Freedoms and Advantages

───── ❧❦ ─────

This has four parts:
1. Identifying the freedoms and advantages
2. The difficulty of gaining the freedoms and advantages
3. The immense significance of gaining them
4. The consequent logic of using them meaningfully

IDENTIFYING THE FREEDOMS AND ADVANTAGES

The freedoms

> By avoiding the eight states with no chance for Dharma practice, freedom will always be gained.

As this quote from the *Precious Verse Summary of the Perfection of Wisdom* states, *freedom* means to be free from the eight states lacking opportunity, which are as follows:

> A hell being, a preta,[44] an animal,
> a barbarian, a long-lived god,
> a holder of wrong views, in a world without a Buddha,
> or incapable of understanding—these are the eight states
>   lacking freedom.

As this says, they consist of *four nonhuman states*: (1–3) in the three lower realms and (4) as a long-lived god residing in one region of the heaven of Great Fruition;[45] and *four human states*: (1) a barbarian and the like in uncivilized lands of border regions, (2) holding wrong views by denying the laws of karma and so on, (3) in a land that lacks the Buddha's teachings, or (4) incapable of understanding or communicating, because of some impairment to the tongue or mental faculty.

These eight states are said to "lack freedom" because they are without the opportunity to practice the Dharma. By contrast, an existence in which these unfree states are avoided is known as "free" or unrestricted because it affords opportunity for Dharma practice.

The advantages

Of the ten advantages, those favorable circumstances for practicing the Dharma that relate to our own individual continuum are referred to as *personal advantages*. There are five of them, as mentioned in these lines:

> A human being, born in a central land, with faculties intact,
> with lifestyle uncorrupted, and with faith in the proper objects.

As this says, the *five personal advantages* are: (1) to be a human being, (2) to be born in a central land where the four types of Buddhist followers (monks, nuns, laymen, and laywomen) are present, (3) to have faculties that are intact and without faults such as speech impairment, (4) to uphold a lifestyle that is uncorrupted, meaning that one has not committed the crimes with immediate retribution and so on, and (5) to have faith in the teachings, which are the source of all virtue and positivity.

Likewise, it is also said:

> A Buddha has come, taught the Dharma,
> these teachings still remain and have followers,
> and there are those who are kind and loving to others.

This says that (1) a Buddha has come to this world, (2) he has taught the sacred Dharma, (3) these teachings still survive, (4) there are other individuals who follow them, and (5) there are benefactors who generously provide food, clothing, and the like to these followers. Since these five favorable circumstances for practicing the Dharma pertain to others, they are referred to as the *circumstantial advantages*.

A physical existence that has these qualities of freedom and advantage is praised again and again in the teachings as being the perfect support for Dharma practice.

THE DIFFICULTY OF GAINING THE FREEDOMS AND ADVANTAGES

In terms of their cause

Generally, it is said that even to gain an existence in the higher realms depends on the cause of carrying out abundant positive actions, and that for someone who lacks virtue and who has committed harmful deeds, it is extremely difficult even to hear the name of higher realms. As it says in Śāntideva's *Introduction to the Bodhisattva's Way of Life* (6:19):

> Once there, never doing any good
> and only amassing harmful deeds,
> not for a hundred million eons
> will I ever hear of happy realms.

Above all, an existence complete with all the perfect freedoms and advantages cannot be attained without accumulating virtue on a vast scale. Any distinction between positive and negative forms of life must arise due to particular causes, namely positive or negative actions.

Since this is so, there are very few beings who possess the cause, which is abundant virtue. As it says in Āryadeva's *Four Hundred Verses* (7:6):

> For the most part, human beings
> cling to unwholesome ways.
> These ordinary beings are therefore
> surely destined for lower realms.

As this says, since most living beings, including humans, are entirely caught up in unwholesome ways, they will surely be drawn to lower realms.

In terms of nature

If we consider the other classes of beings, even a basic human existence is as rare as a star in broad daylight. Living beings of the six classes, it is said, come into existence on a vast scale, like masses of grains. If we consider only those animals who wander on the surface of the earth, and only those in plain sight, we can verify this through our own experience. If we think how many creatures can be seen, whether on land or in water, just in our own field of vision, or how many living organisms exist within our own body, we can immediately realize just how slim is the chance of gaining a human body. What need is there to mention therefore how difficult it is to gain a human body complete with all the freedoms and advantages?

In this respect, we can consider that even during eons of light—as opposed to the eons of darkness in which even the word "*buddha*" is not heard—there are still some places that are pervaded by the light of the sacred Dharma and some that are not. Even if we are born in a land where the Dharma has reached, there is still a difference between those who are suitable vessels for the teachings and those who are not. Then, even the suitable must first come across the teachings and a spiritual guide who can teach them, and having met them, they must be inspired and then set out upon the path, and having embarked on the path, complete it. If we consider just how rare this is, we might compare it to an *udumbara*[46] flower. In consideration of this point, the *Gaṇḍavyūha Sūtra* says:

> It is rare to escape the eight states lacking opportunity.
> It is rare to become a human being.
> It is rare to find perfect freedom.
> It is rare for a buddha to appear...

The text continues in some detail. We also find the following lines in the Perfection of Wisdom sūtras:

> Friends, it is rare to find perfect freedom. It is rare to be born a human being.

By means of an example
Śāntideva's *Introduction to the Bodhisattva's Way of Life* (4:20) says:

> That is why the Lord Buddha has said that,
> hard as it might be for a turtle to place
> its neck through a yoke adrift upon the ocean,
> extremely difficult it is to gain a human life.

As this says, the sūtras tell us that it is as difficult to gain a human body as it is for a one-eyed turtle living in the ocean's depths, and rising to its surface only once every hundred years, to place its neck through a yoke that is floating upon the surface and blown by the wind in all directions.

THE IMMENSE SIGNIFICANCE OF GAINING THEM

This physical existence, which is so difficult to obtain, is extremely significant, for it can be used to cross over the river of suffering. As it says in *Introduction to the Bodhisattva's Way of Life* (7:14):

> Take advantage of this boat, the human body,
> to free yourself from the great river of suffering.
> Since this boat will be hard to find again,
> now is not the time for sleep, you fool!

In practicing the Mahāyāna path especially, a support such as this is highly praised. As it says in Candragomin's *Letter to a Disciple* (verse 64):

The path followed and taught by the Buddha in order to guide
    the world
is within the reach of human beings with strength of heart,
but cannot be attained by gods, nāgas,
asuras, garuḍas, vidyādharas, kiṃnaras, or uragas.[47]

THE CONSEQUENT LOGIC OF USING THEM MEANINGFULLY

Given that this physical existence—which is so difficult to find and
yet so potentially significant—enables us to accomplish liberation and
omniscience, it is of even greater value to us than a wish-fulfilling jewel.
Once we understand this, it is only logical that we will put our energy
into making it meaningful.

Letter to a Disciple (verse 63) says:

Having found this state, we can escape the ocean of rebirth
and sow the virtuous seeds of supreme awakening.
This human life is more valuable even than
    a wishing-gem—
who could let it go to waste and fail to bear its fruit?

Having gained this perfect human existence, to use it for harmful
actions is described as the most foolish thing one could possibly do. As
Nāgārjuna's *Letter to a Friend* (verse 60) puts it:

Even more stupid than one who cleans up vomit
with a golden vase bedecked with jewels
is the one who, having been born a human,
devotes his life to committing harmful deeds.

And *Introduction to the Bodhisattva's Way of Life* (4:23) says:

Having found freedom such as this,
if I do not then train myself in virtue,

what greater deception could there be?
What folly could compare with this?

We might think that rather than devoting this *present* existence to virtuous actions, we will do so in lives to come, but that would be a mistake. As *Introduction to the Bodhisattva's Way of Life* (4:17) tells us:

And with a lifestyle such as this,
I'll never again find a human body;
and if a human form is not attained,
there will be only harm, never virtue.

Those who are bereft of positive conduct will be unable to gain the higher realms at all. Moreover, with a form in the lower realms, they will find it impossible to cultivate a wealth of virtue and will instead be overcome by suffering and negativity. *Introduction to the Bodhisattva's Way of Life* (4:18) also says:

Now I have the chance to practice virtue,
but if I do not act in wholesome ways,
then what shall I do when bewildered
by all the misery of the lower realms?

❧❧

Reflect again and again on the reasons as to why this body, with its freedoms and advantages, is difficult to obtain, why it is of great significance, and why it is wise to make full use of it. Make the firm decision that you will devote yourself to the Dharma as the way to make this life meaningful. And since it is certain that the supreme Dharma is bodhicitta in both its aspects, put all your heart and soul into making it arise, remain, and increase. As a way to remain mindful of this you can recite the following verse from *Introduction to the Bodhisattva's Way of Life* (1:4) and contemplate its meaning:

This free and well-favored human form is difficult to obtain.
Now that you have the chance to realize the full human
    potential,
if you don't make good use of this opportunity,
how could you possibly expect to have such a chance again?

Extremely difficult to obtain, this support for many qualities,
   this boat for crossing over the great river of suffering,
greater than a wish-granting jewel, this human form, free and well-favored—
    intelligent ones, how could you not employ it
     for your own and others' good?

4. Death and Impermanence

꧁ ꧂

This is divided into three sections: reflecting on the certainty of death, the uncertainty of the time of death, and how nothing aside from the Dharma can help us at the time of death.

THE CERTAINTY OF DEATH

This has three parts: death is inevitable, life cannot be extended but is always diminishing, and we cannot avoid death through circumstances.

Death is inevitable.

Generally all conditioned things are subject to four eventualities. As a sūtra says:

> Meeting must end in separation,
> prosperity must end in decline,
> all that is gathered will be dispersed,
> and life must end in death.

It is therefore needless to point out that this human body—weak and fragile as it is—will not last. As we find in Nāgārjuna's *Letter to a Friend* (verse 57):

The ground, Mount Meru, and the oceans too
will be consumed by seven blazing suns.
And of things with form not even ashes will remain—
what need to mention human beings, frail as they are?

You might think that this applies only to some but will not necessarily
befall us all. However, that is not so. As Aśvaghoṣa's *Letter of Consolation* says:

Have you ever, on earth or in the heavens,
seen a being who was born never to die?
Have you heard that this has happened?
Or even suspected that it might?

As these quotations indicate, death is inevitable for all who have been
born. We should therefore reflect on this by means of examples, such as
those given in the following quotation from the *Lalitavistara Sūtra*:

This existence of ours is as transient as autumn clouds.
To watch the birth and death of beings is like looking at the
    movement of a dance.
A lifetime is like a flash of lightning in the sky,
rushing by, like a torrent down a steep mountain.

Life cannot be extended but is always diminishing.
From the moment we first enter the womb, we do not pause for even a
moment but move ever closer to the clutches of the Lord of Death. As
a sūtra says:

O bravest of men, from that very first night
when a person takes his place in the womb,
from then on, every day, without pause,
he gets closer and closer to the Lord of Death.

You might think that this is not true for vidyādharas and others who have gained the attainment (*siddhi*) of longevity so it is not true for everybody. But this is not so: although they may live long, these masters too must eventually die. *Letter of Consolation* says:

> Great rishis with the five superknowledges
> can fly far and wide through the sky,
> yet they will never reach a place
> where they will live on and never die.

As this says, even great rishis with extraordinary powers of clairvoyance must eventually face death. What is more, even the emanated form (*nirmāṇakāya*) of the buddhas demonstrates impermanence. So what need is there to mention other beings, propelled as they are by the force of their past actions?

The same text says:

> If even the indestructible body of the buddhas,
> adorned with major and minor marks,
> does not last forever,
> what need is there to mention other beings,
> whose bodies are as insubstantial as plantain trees?

Therefore, since our lives, which are propelled by our past actions, do not increase but diminish constantly, without a moment's pause, death is certain. As it says in Śāntideva's *Introduction to the Bodhisattva's Way of Life* (2:39):

> Never halting, day or night,
> my life is always slipping by.
> Having gone, life cannot be extended,
> so how could the likes of me not die?

We cannot avoid death through circumstances.

You might wonder: Can death be avoided through some method such as the use of mantra or medicine? It cannot. When the time of death has arrived, it cannot be averted by any circumstances whatsoever.

The *Sūtra of Instructions to the King* says:

> Your majesty, it is like this. Imagine that from all four directions there appears a great mass of gemstones in the sky. The gems are extremely tough and solid, utterly unbreakable, indestructible, unyielding, and hard. Gathering together in four groups in the sky and then falling to the earth below, they crush to dust all the plants and trees, together with their branches, stalks, and leaves, and all animals and living creatures. This would not be easy to escape through fleetness, to avert through strength, or to avoid through use of special substances, mantras, or medicine. Your majesty, in the same way, these four great fears will come, and difficult it will be to escape them through fleetness, or to avert them through strength, or to avoid them through the use of special substances, mantras, or medicine. What are these four? They are aging, sickness, decline, and death. Your majesty, aging comes upon us and destroys our youth. Sickness comes upon us and destroys our good health. Decline comes upon us and destroys our prosperity and success. Death comes upon us and destroys our life. It is not easy to escape these through fleetness, to avert them through strength, or to avoid them through the use of special substances, mantras, or medicine.

Contemplate the certainty of death by reflecting on these three themes and arrive at a firm decision to practice Dharma.

THE UNCERTAINTY OF THE TIME OF DEATH

This has three parts: the lifespan of beings in this world of ours is not fixed, there are many causes of death and few for sustaining life, and even the causes for sustaining life can become causes of death.

The lifespan of beings in this world of ours is not fixed.

The lifespan of beings in this world of Jambudvīpa is extremely uncertain. Vasubandhu's *Treasury of Abhidharma* (3:79):

> It is uncertain: at the end it's ten years,
> and in the beginning it's incalculable.

As this says, lifespan is not fixed, because eventually it will reach only ten years while in the beginning human beings were capable of living countless years. Human beings of this day and age in particular grow old and frail after approximately sixty years, but we can see directly how, due to various adverse conditions, both outer and inner, many die without completing their allotted span of life. A sūtra says:

> Some die old and some die young,
> some die in the prime of youth,
> some die before they learn to crawl,
> and some die even in the womb.

There are many causes of death and few for sustaining life.

Nāgārjuna's *Precious Garland* (4:17) says:

> The Lord of Death awaits, close at hand,
> as you live, like a candle in the wind.

Like a candle in the breeze, any number of adverse circumstances could bring about our deaths, and we would be powerless to prevent them. There is nothing whatsoever about our lives that is reliable. There are countless conditions and circumstances that could steal away our lives:

external influences including human and nonhuman beings, the elements of earth, water, fire, and wind, and so on, and internal conditions such as illness caused by an imbalance in the three humors of wind, bile, and phlegm. As it is said in the *Great Parinirvāṇa Sūtra*:

> Our life is always threatened by countless enemies—
> with each passing moment it diminishes,
> and it cannot possibly be extended.

Even causes for sustaining life can become causes of death.

We can see for ourselves that sometimes even those things we presume to sustain life, such as food and clothing, our homes, friends, and relatives and the like can become causes of death. And some, driven crazy by harmful influences or despair, even use poison or weapons to take their own lives. So, since even causes for sustaining life can certainly become causes of death, the time of our death is far from certain. The *Precious Garland* (3:78) says:

> Causes of death are numerous,
> while causes of life are few indeed,
> and even those may cause death;
> so practice Dharma at all times.

Contemplate the uncertainty of the time of death by reflecting on these three themes, and arrive at a firm decision that you will practice the Dharma this very instant, without putting it off until later.

How nothing aside from the Dharma can help us at the time of death

This has three parts: our possessions cannot help us, our friends and relatives cannot help us, and our body cannot help us.

Our possessions cannot help us.

When we die, we must give up all the various possessions we have so painstakingly acquired during our lives, and we will not even be able to look at them, so what need is there to mention that they will not be of any benefit. The *Sūtra of Instructions to the King* explains this in detail. It says:

> Your majesty, it is like this. Imagine a man or a woman who sleeps and dreams of delightful gardens, magnificent mountains, pleasant forests, beautiful rivers, attractive ponds, fine estates, and splendid mansions. Upon waking, he or she does not see any of them. Your majesty, in the same way, your kingdom, your life, the pleasures of your realm, the pleasures of royal power, the pleasures of satisfying desire, and the pleasures of all your desirable possessions are just like the contents of a dream.
>
> Your majesty, it is like this. Your elephants, horses, chariots, infantry, wives, homes, consorts, ministers, astrologers, closest advisors, bodyguards, attendants, parents, siblings, children, male and female servants, workers, volunteers, friends, relatives, countrymen, money, gold, jewels, pearls, sapphires, conches, crystals, corals, refined gold, silver, clothes, ornaments, pantries, granaries, and storehouses and the rest must all be left behind. They are all impermanent, unstable, and unreliable. They are changing and short-lived. They do not remain as they are; they fluctuate. They are transient and momentary, and ultimately unwholesome. They lead to loss and dispersal. They perish in the end. They will ultimately be dispersed, but in the meantime they bring all manner of fear, harm, anguish, and strife. They cause loss and downfall. They will be divided up, separated, and destroyed. They will disintegrate entirely.
>
> Your majesty, you should therefore regard them as impermanent and as leading to loss and dispersal, and since you will die, be fearful. Your majesty, let the Dharma alone be your kingdom. Since these are not the Dharma, do not pursue them. Act in accordance with the Dharma. Do not do anything that is incompatible with the Dharma.

Our friends and relatives cannot help us.

When we are tormented by the feeling of our life being taken away, even if we are surrounded by thousands of friends and relatives, all of them valiant and courageous, they will be quite incapable of helping us in even the slightest way. They will not be able to take away even a small fraction of the pain of dying, nor extend our lives, nor guide us on our journey. We must experience all the pain of death and dying by ourselves. As it says in *Introduction to the Bodhisattva's Way of Life* (2:40–41):

> While I lie there in my final bed,
> friends and family may be by my side,
> but I alone will be the one
> to feel the severing of all ties to life.
>
> When I'm seized by the emissaries of Death,
> what help will be my family or my friends?
> At that time it's merit alone that can protect me,
> but upon that, alas, I have failed to depend.

Our body cannot help us.

When the time comes to leave this world for the next, the body of this present life will not be able to help us in the slightest, and even while the consciousness of the intermediate state (*bardo*) wanders without support, we will not be able to use this body as a vessel even for a day.

As the same text (8:31) says:

> This body arose as a whole,
> but its flesh and bones
> will break up and separate.
> So what need to mention friends?

In short, we must know that the Lord of Death will certainly come, but when he will come is uncertain. When we understand how he is, in this sense, unreliable, it is only right for us to curtail our plans and preparations for this life. As the same text (2:33) says:

> The Lord of Death is fickle, unworthy of our trust;
> whether life's tasks are done or not, he will not wait.
> For the sick and for the healthy alike,
> this fleeting life is not a thing on which we can rely.

And it (7:5) also says:

> One by one, he's taken all your kind,
> yet perhaps you have not noticed?
> For still you go on resting idly by,
> like cattle sleeping at the butcher's feet.

Though we may spend our time carelessly asleep or resting idly, which are only inferior forms of conduct, the Lord of Death will arrive suddenly, without any concern as to whether or not we have finished what we have begun. When this happens, we will be tortured by regret. As the same text (7:8) says:

> When I've not done this, and this is barely started,
> and this is only halfway through,
> then the Lord of Death will suddenly arrive,
> and I will think, "Oh no, I am no more!"

At that time, even if we think we must devote ourselves to the Dharma, it will not be possible, because the mind will be too disturbed by all the pain of dying, and with time running out, there will be no opportunity. As Śāntideva (7:9–10) says:

> Their eyes red and swollen
> and their faces stained with tears,
> your loved ones will finally lose hope
> as you glimpse the messengers of Death.

When remembering your past wrongs
and when hearing hellish sounds,
you will soil yourself in terror;
delirious, whatever will you do?

Therefore, by reflecting along these lines, we must firmly decide that we will not leave Dharma practice to chance. It is certain that we will die, and at the time of death, nothing but Dharma will afford us refuge or protection. This point is expressed very clearly in the *Sūtra of Instructions to the King*:

> Your majesty, it is like this. The lion, king of beasts, enters into a herd of other animals and captures one as it pleases. When that poor creature is caught in the lion's terrible jaws, it is powerless to resist. Your majesty, in just the same way, when we are impaled on the stake of the Lord of Death, there will be no room for complacency. We will have no protection, no refuge, and no defender.
>
> Our condition will be destroyed, our joints torn apart, our flesh and blood dried up, our body tormented with sickness, our mouth dry, and our expression changed. Our limbs will flail about, and we will be powerless, unable to act. We will stain our bodies with tears, mucus, urine, and feces. Our senses—eyes, ears, nose, tongue, and body—and the mental faculty will cease to function. We will hiccup uncontrollably and cry out in a harsh, rasping voice. The doctors will desert us. We will have no appetite for medicine, food, or drink. We will lie in our very last bed, before departing for another destination.
>
> We will fall into the beginningless cycle of birth, aging, and death. Only a fraction of our life force will be left. We will be frightened by the henchman of the Lord of Death and fall prey to misery. The movement of our breath will cease. Our mouth will hang open, our nostrils flared and our teeth tightly clenched. We will pray for some kind of redemption. Our karmic propensities will be transferred to our future

existence. We will be utterly alone, without friend or companion. We will leave this world behind.

We will go on to the next world. We will move on. We will enter the great darkness. We will fall into the great abyss. We will enter the great charnel ground. We will set out into the great wilderness. We will be swept away by the great ocean. We will be carried along by the winds of karma. We will journey to the place without rest. We will enter the great battlefield. We will be caught by the great demon. We will clutch helplessly at the sky.[48] We will be surrounded by our parents, brothers, sisters, sons, and daughters, all congregated around us. Our breathing will grow shorter. We will hear talk of our belongings being divided. In anguish and despair, we will call out to our mother, our father, and our children, and we will pull our hair.

At such a time, only generosity, spiritual practice, and the teachings will help us. Nothing but the Dharma will protect us. There will be no other refuge, no other defender. Your majesty, at that time, the Dharma will be like a sanctuary, a safe haven, or a guide in whom we can place our trust.

By recollecting death in these ways, we will know the happiness and suffering of this life to be just like a flash of lightning in the sky, or like the happiness and suffering of a dream. As it says in *Introduction to the Bodhisattva's Way of Life* (6:57–58):

> Suppose a person should awaken from a dream
> in which he knew a hundred years of happiness,
> while another person awakens from a dream
> in which he experienced just a moment's joy.

> For both these dreamers, now awake,
> happiness has gone, never to return.
> Likewise, when the time of death arrives,
> our lives, however long or short, are over.

Therefore, we must turn our minds away from the pursuit of this life's fleeting pleasures and keep the pursuit of long-term happiness and virtue deep within our hearts. Knowing that there is no better method for this than bodhicitta, we must put all our energy into contemplating ways to arouse, sustain, and increase it. In order to keep these points in our thoughts, we can recite these words from the *Sūtra on Impermanence*:

> Good health does not last; youth does not last;
> prosperity does not last; even life itself does not last.
> When a person, who is by nature impermanent,
> indulges the senses, how could that bring joy?

Contemplate the meaning of these lines.

⁓⁊ ⁊⁓

> *Alas, it is certain that the fearsome Lord of Death will take me,*
> *terrified and alone, and powerless to resist.*
> *At that time, nothing but the Dharma will protect me—*
> *intelligent friends, set your minds upon the Dharma!*

5. Actions and Their Effects

─── ❦ ───

When we are certain about all that is explained here, whether or not we act on it and take up the Dharma will depend on our intention, the aspiration toward the Dharma. And the arising of this aspiration depends on contemplating the effects of our actions. As Śāntideva's *Introduction to the Bodhisattva's Way of Life* (7:40) says:

> Aspiration, so the Sage has said,
> is the root of every kind of virtue.
> And the root of aspiration is meditating
> constantly on the fruits of action.

This section has two parts: contemplating the effects of actions in general and contemplating specific types of action.

CONTEMPLATING THE EFFECTS OF ACTIONS IN GENERAL

This has two parts: the certainty of karma, and the proliferation of effects.

The certainty of karma

A sūtra says:

When his time has come, even a king has to die,
and neither his friends nor his wealth can follow him.
So for us—wherever we stay, wherever we go—
karma follows us like a shadow.

When we enter the next life, it is certain that we will be accompanied only by our positive and negative actions. It is also certain that we ourselves will be the ones to experience the results of whatever actions we have accumulated; these results will not ripen on others. A sūtra says:

> The actions that we have done and accumulated
> will not ripen externally upon the earth,
> nor will they ripen in the water or fire or wind,
> they will not ripen in the expanse of space,
> but will ripen in our aggregates, in our own experience.

And the *King of Samādhi Sūtra* says:

> Having carried out an action, you cannot avoid its result,
> and you will not experience what has been done by others.

Why? It is said that the results of our actions will not go to waste, and we will not face the results of acts we have not committed.

We might feel it is uncertain that actions performed a long time ago will still produce results. But any karma that has not been rendered ineffective by adverse factors will not disappear simply because a long time has passed. When the right circumstances come together, it will surely bear its fruit. As the *Hundred Actions* tells us:

> The actions of beings never go to waste,
> even after a hundred eons;
> when the conditions are assembled,
> they will certainly bear fruit.

As for the order in which actions ripen, the Sthavira Rāhulabhadra[49] says:

> Whichever actions carry the greatest effect,
> whichever are closest, whichever most habitual,
> and whichever were done first—
> these will be the very first to ripen.

That is to say, strongest actions will be the first to ripen. If actions are of equal strength, that which is more recent and clearest in the mind at the time of death will ripen first. If they are equal in this respect as well, it will be whichever action is most habitual; and if equal too in this respect, whichever action was done first will be the first to ripen.

The proliferation of effects

Although we may be certain about the effects of major positive or negative actions, we might think that minor actions do not bring about effects. But that is not so, because inner causality involves vast proliferation. As it says in the *Collection of Meaningful Expressions*:

> Even a small misdeed
> can bring terrors in the next life
> and lead eventually to ruin,
> just like poison in the stomach.
>
> Even a small good deed
> can bring great joy in the next life
> and the fulfillment of great purpose,
> just like crops produced from grain.

Certainty with regard to this can be gained by recalling the stories of the nāga king Elapatra[50] and King Māndhātri,[51] and how great results come from minor causes.

Well, you might wonder, what is the difference between great and small? Nāgārjuna's *Letter to a Friend* (verse 42):

> Constancy, motivation, lack of counteragent,
> and the field of excellence—these determine
> the five kinds of major virtue and nonvirtue.
> Of these, strive for conduct that is virtuous.

As this says, actions performed constantly, with a strong motivation, without remedies such as regret that would cancel them out, and arising from a field of excellence, such as the Three Jewels, or the teacher, or from a field of benefit, such as one's parents, are major actions. Their opposites are minor actions.

Moreover, premeditated actions are referred to as "committed and accumulated," whereas unintentional acts are said to be "committed but not accumulated."

Introduction to the Bodhisattva's Way of Life (5:81) says:

> Constantly inspired by a strong motivation
> or motivated by the remedial forces,
> actions before the fields of excellence, benefit
> or misery, become major deeds of virtue.

And Vasubandhu's *Treasury of Abhidharma* (4:119) says:

> The conclusion,[52] field, and basis,
> the preparation and the intention—
> according to whether these are great or small,
> the action itself will be great or small.

CONTEMPLATING SPECIFIC TYPES OF ACTION

This is divided into two parts: contemplating negative actions and contemplating positive actions.

Contemplating negative actions

This has three parts: contemplating (1) the actions and (2) their effects, and (3) avoiding them.

CONTEMPLATING THE ACTIONS

Although, generally speaking, there are unimaginable varieties of positive and negative actions, we can summarize them, as the *Treasury of Abhidharma* (4:66) says:

> Summarizing the most evident of these,
> there are said to be ten courses of action,
> virtuous and nonvirtuous respectively.

As this says, there are principally ten forms of negative action, consisting of:

- Three of the *body*: taking life, taking what is not given, and sexual misconduct
- Four of the *speech*: lying, divisive talk, harsh speech, and idle gossip
- Three of the *mind*: covetousness, malice, and wrong view

Their respective natures are described in the *Treasury of Abhidharma* (4:73–74):

> Taking life is to kill another,
> deliberately and without error.
> Taking what is not given is to appropriate,
> by force or stealth, another's possessions.
> Sexual misconduct is to have intercourse
> lustfully and with an unsuitable partner.
> Lying is to speak while believing the opposite
> to someone who comprehends one's speech.

And (4:76):

> Divisive talk is to cause others to separate
> through speech motivated by destructive emotions.
> Harsh speech is to use unpleasant words.
> Gossip includes all talk motivated by destructive emotions.

And (4:77–78):

> Covetousness is to desire others' wealth.
> Malice is to feel hatred toward beings.
> Wrong view is to deny right and wrong.
> Three are courses of action; seven are also action.

As this says, these can be understood in terms of basis, intention, execution, and completion.

Moreover, the three poisonous destructive emotions and actions motivated by them are called *nonvirtuous*. As Nāgārjuna's *Precious Garland* (1:20) says:

> Desire, anger, and delusion
> and actions arising from them are nonvirtuous.

CONTEMPLATING EFFECTS

Each of these types of negative conduct has its own fully ripened effect, effect resembling the cause, and ruling effect. As it says in the *Treasury of Abhidharma* (4:85):

> Everything is said to bring forth its ruling,
> cause-resembling, and fully ripened effects.

Fully Ripened Effect

According to the scale of an action and the motivation behind it, we might be reborn among the three lower realms, such as the hells, or in the higher realms, but with physical and mental suffering. The *Precious Garland* (1:21) says:

> From nonvirtue comes all suffering
> and all the lower realms too.

And (3:29):

Through desire, we will go to the hungry ghost (*preta*) realm.
Through anger, we will be flung into the hells.
Through delusion, we will become an animal.

And *Introduction to the Bodhisattva's Way of Life* (7:41) says:

Physical suffering, unhappiness,
and all the various kinds of fear
as well as separation from what we desire
all arise from an unwholesome way of life.

And (7:43):

Acting negatively, we may wish for happiness,
but no matter where we go,
we will always, as a result of our wrongdoing,
be destroyed by the weapons of suffering.

And (7:45):

As a result of my many wrongs, I will be brought low, my skin
    flayed off by Yama's minions,
liquid bronze, melted in the hottest fires, poured upon
    my body,
pierced by burning swords and knives, and my flesh split
into a hundred pieces, falling upon the ground of white-hot iron.

You might doubt this, as there are some who do wrong but still appear to be happy. Yet such doubts are out of place, for their happiness is also the result of positive deeds they have done in the past, whereas the effects of present negative actions will mostly be experienced after death. Nāgārjuna's *Letter to a Friend* (verse 31) tells us:

Although acting in wrong and harmful ways
does not hurt us, like a weapon, right away,

when the time of death is upon us,
the results of harmful actions will be clear.

Effects Similar to the Cause

(1) *Experiences similar to the cause* mean that even if, due to some other actions, we are reborn as human beings, we will experience a short life and so on. The *Precious Garland* (1:14–16) puts it like this:

> By taking life, our own life will be curtailed.
> Violence will bring much harm upon us.
> Through stealing we will lack possessions.
> Through adultery we will encounter rivals.
>
> Speaking falsely will cause us to face slander.
> Divisive talk will separate us from our friends.
> Through harsh speech we'll hear unpleasant words.
> Incoherent talk will mean our speech is not respected.
>
> Covetousness will destroy our hopes.
> Malice will bring us many fears.
> And wrong view will bring inferior beliefs.

(2) *Actions similar to the cause* means that we will continue to act just as we have in the past, or in similar ways.

The Ruling Effects

This refers to all kinds of hostile effects in our outer environment and circumstances, such as our possessions being unimpressive, there being too much or too little precipitation, and so on. As the same text also says:

> Externally, there will be little prosperity and many hailstorms,
> swirling dust, smells, undulating terrain,
> salt plains, and erratic seasons.
> Harvests will be minimal or nonexistent.[53]

CONTEMPLATION ON AVOIDING THESE ACTIONS

When we are certain that unwholesome actions produce suffering as their result, we must confess, by means of the four powers,[54] all the harms that we have done in the past, and vow never to act harmfully again, even at the cost of our lives. As it says in *Letter to a Friend* (verse 88):

> The seeds of these, the effects of nonvirtue,
> are harmful actions of body, speech, and mind.
> Strive therefore, and muster all your skill,
> to avoid even the slightest such misdeeds.

And *Introduction to the Bodhisattva's Way of Life* (1:62) says:

> How can I free myself from nonvirtue,
> the source from which sufferings arise?
> At all times of the day and night
> this should be my one concern.

You might wonder whether it is permissible to act in harmful ways for the sake of friends or relatives. It is not. *Letter to a Friend* (verse 30) provides the reason:

> Do not act harmfully for the sake of monks,
> brahmans, gods, honored guests,
> your parents, queen, or those around you—
> the result in hell will not be shared.

Contemplating positive actions

This has three parts: contemplating (1) the actions and (2) their effects, and (3) adopting them.

CONTEMPLATING THE ACTIONS

The intention and the practice of avoiding the ten ways of negative conduct mentioned above comprise the ten principal forms of virtuous action. As the *Precious Garland* (1:8–9) says:

Not killing, not stealing,
renouncing others' wives,
refraining entirely from false,
divisive, harsh, and senseless speech,
avoiding all covetousness and malice
and the views of the nihilists—
these are the ten ways of positive action.

Moreover, actions committed in the absence of the three poisons and motivated by faith and the like are described as virtues or positive deeds. As the same text (1:20) says:

Non-desire, non-hatred, non-ignorance
and the actions they generate are virtues.

And (1:10):

Not drinking alcohol, leading an ethical life,
avoiding harm, giving to others respectfully,
honoring the worthy, and being loving—
this, in short, is the practice of Dharma.

CONTEMPLATING THEIR EFFECTS
The fully ripened effects are the opposites of those described above for the nonvirtues. As the same text (1:19) says:

Whatever effects are described
for the so-called "nonvirtues,"
in the case of the virtues
it is their opposites that occur.

And (1:21):

From virtues come higher realms
and happiness in all lives.

And (1:23–24):

> Through these practices, we will be freed from the hells
> and the realms of pretas and animals.
> Among gods and human beings,
> we will find happiness, fortune, and dominion.
> Through the concentrations, immeasurables, and formless
>   meditations,
> we will experience the bliss of Brahmā and so forth.

The attitude and the conduct of the Mahāyāna in particular will yield its own results. As the same text (5:38) says:

> Generosity brings wealth, discipline happiness,
> patience yields an attractive form, diligence glory,
> meditation brings peace, and wisdom liberation.
> Compassion brings the fulfillment of all wishes.

In short, we can be certain that the cause of all the happiness of the higher realms and the definite goodness of liberation is nothing other than virtuous action. As Śāntideva's *Introduction to the Bodhisattva's Way of Life* (7:42) tells us:

> Through virtuous deeds, well considered,
> then no matter where I go,
> there I will be honored
> by the results of all my merit.

CONTEMPLATION ON ADOPTING THESE ACTIONS

When we are certain about this causal relationship, we must strive to carry out virtuous deeds however we can, in both thought and deed. As the same text (7:46) says:

> Therefore I will aspire toward virtue
> and train myself in it devotedly.

And *Letter to a Friend* (verse 5) says:

> Constantly apply yourself with body, speech, and mind
> to these ten ways of virtuous conduct.
> Refrain from alcohol and
> take delight in a wholesome way of life.

With knowledge of what must be adopted, we must take up these actions constantly and devotedly, without relying on anything or anyone else at all. As it says in *Introduction to the Bodhisattva's Way of Life* (5:82):

> With knowledge and with faith,
> I shall constantly undertake these deeds.
> And in whatever actions I perform,
> I shall not depend on others.

Moreover, we should also understand the cause and effect of neutral actions and the cause and effect of partially positive, partially negative actions, and for specifically positive or negative actions, the distinction between propelling karma and completing karma, and the distinction between karma experienced in this life, the next life, or in subsequent lives, or karma that is uncertain to be experienced. With this understanding, we must strive to transform neutral actions into positive ones and so on, adopting whatever must be adopted and avoiding whatever must be avoided.

In particular, we must purify the most serious of negative actions, including wrong view—which destroys the sources of our virtue—as well as anger and forsaking the Dharma. We must confess such actions, vow never to repeat them in the future, and put our energy into applying the most powerful antidotes. This is a crucial instruction.

In short, it says in Sakya Paṇḍita's *Clear Differentiation of the Three Sets of Vows* (1:42–43):

> Virtue is wholesome practice

and brings happiness as its result.
Nonvirtue is unwholesome practice
and brings suffering as its result.

As this says, we must always maintain a correct view, certain of the effects of both positive and negative action. If we have this, we will possess the vital artery leading to the higher realms and liberation. But without it, we will have nothing. *Letter to a Friend* (verse 47) has this to say:

If you wish to reach higher states and liberation,
become familiar with the correct view.
Someone whose view is incorrect, even if acting positively,
will experience only unbearable results.

Once we gain certainty about the general and particular effects of our actions, we will certainly take pains to adopt even the slightest positive actions and to avoid even the slightest negative ones. Most importantly, we will strive to ensure that precious bodhicitta arises, remains, and increases. To stay mindful of this, we should recite verses such as the following, which is from the *Moon Lamp Sūtra*, and reflect on their meaning:

Actions, once performed, will not come to nothing.
Positive or negative, they will bear fruit accordingly.
This doorway to the way of reasoning is excellent,
subtle, and hard to see, for it lies within the buddhas' purview.

❦

With certainty gained through infallible logic
concerning the specific effects of deeds, both positive and negative,
which are like fruits born of medicinal or poisonous seeds,
to adopt and avoid with diligence—this is the heart of the Dharma.

6. The Trials of Saṃsāra

—❦❦—

This has two parts: reflecting on the trials of saṃsāra in general and reflecting on the trials of particular realms.

REFLECTING ON THE TRIALS OF SAṂSĀRA IN GENERAL

This has three parts: reflecting on the three sufferings, the six sufferings, and the eight sufferings.

The three sufferings

Unless we understand the general trials of saṃsāra, we will not feel inspired to strive for freedom. As we find in Āryadeva's *Four Hundred Verses* (8:12):

> Unless you are weary with this,
> how could you take interest in peace?

Therefore, in order to generate a sense of weariness with the whole of conditioned existence, the source of all our suffering, it is right to reflect on the trials of saṃsāra. As Nāgārjuna's *Letter to a Friend* (verse 65) says:

> Develop disenchantment with saṃsāra,
> the source of many pains,
> including frustration of desires, death, sickness, and old age.
> Pay heed to its defects, even just a few.[55]

When the intelligent examine it well, they find that the whole of saṃsāra is characterized by suffering and there is nowhere we might avoid it. Some experience suffering upon suffering, some experience the suffering of change, and everyone experiences the suffering of conditioning. As it says in Vasubandhu's *Treasury of Abhidharma* (6:3):

> Suffering from the three types of suffering,
> all—whatever their kind—are suffering.

The majority of beings in the lower realms such as the hells are afflicted by *suffering upon suffering*, which means that they are tormented physically and mentally as more and more suffering is piled upon their existing pains. It is like contracting leprosy and then having the further pain of ulcerous sores, or like the sting of salt water when applied to a wound.

The majority of beings in the higher realms, such as human beings and the gods of the desire realm, are afflicted by the *suffering of change*, as their prosperity declines, meetings end in separation, and whatever has been gathered is dispersed. All the while, whatever we presume to be happiness turns out to be nothing but the causes and conditions of suffering. The example given here is of eating the wrong amount of food.

Everyone throughout the whole of saṃsāra, from the summit of existence downward, is constantly afflicted by the *pervasive suffering of conditioning* and dysfunctional tendencies. This is because they have not gone beyond tainted causes and effects. The example given for this is of poison in the body.

Still, the spiritually immature who are ignorant of reality continue to regard everything as pure, blissful, lasting, possessing self-identity, and so on. This is because their minds are disturbed by the perverse attachment that is the source of all ruin. Their erroneous perception is similar to the appearance of falling hairs that occurs to people with defective vision. *Letter to a Friend* (verse 48) says:

> Those who lack the foundation of mindfulness
> view things in four mistaken ways and face ruin.

And, referring to the suffering of conditioning in particular, a sūtra says:

> Ordinary beings are like the palm of the hand—
> not noticing the hair of the suffering of conditioning.
> The spiritually advanced are like the eye—
> they are extremely responsive to it.

If we consider the suffering of conditioning as like a strand of hair, the minds of ordinary beings are only as sensitive as the palm, whereas the minds of ārya beings are as keenly sensitive as the surface of the eye.[56]

The six sufferings

THE DISTRESS OF UNCERTAINTY REGARDING FRIEND AND FOE

For beings of the three worlds, there is no certainty about the status of friends and enemies, not only from one lifetime to the next but even in the earlier and later parts of a single lifetime. Sometimes a dear friend or a relative whom we have tried to care for lovingly can turn into a bitter and murderous rival. As *Letter to a Friend* (verse 66) tells us:

> A father can be reborn as a son, a mother as a wife,
> those who were once enemies can become friends;
> and the reverse of such situations can occur as well.
> There's no certainty, therefore, in samsaric states.

THE DISTRESS OF LACKING CONTENTMENT WITH POSSESSIONS

Those whose minds are filled with craving can never find satisfaction or contentment from their material possessions. Each and every one of us has, in the course of beginningless existence, suckled more milk from our mothers' breasts than all the water in four great oceans, yet still we are not satisfied. As the same text (verse 67) says:

> Every being has drunk a volume of milk
> greater than four vast oceans, and yet,

still, in lives to come within saṃsāra,
they will drink even more than this.

THE DISTRESS OF ABANDONING THE BODY AGAIN AND AGAIN

In saṃsāra we have had to experience the distress of forsaking our former bodies infinite times. If we were to pile up the bones of our former bodies—only those that we ourselves have had—they would exceed in size the cosmic mountain. As the same text (verse 68) says:

> The piles of bones from our own previous existences
> would be even greater in size than the cosmic mountain.

THE DISTRESS OF TAKING UP COUNTLESS FURTHER EXISTENCES

The number of times we have taken up a further existence is also without limit. If we tried to count the number of mothers that we ourselves have had, it would be impossible. The same text (verse 68) says:

> There is not enough soil in the world to make a tiny pellet,
> the size of a *kolāsita* berry, for each of your past mothers.

THE DISTRESS OF THE VICISSITUDES OF STATUS AND SO FORTH

For a time we might experience the bliss of the higher realms, but this is unreliable, and although we might be gods or human beings with wealth and splendor in abundance, in time we will experience the various ills of the lower realms. As the same text (verse 69) says:

> Having been Indra, who is praised by all the world,
> the force of karma will pull us down to earth again.
> And having been a wheel-turning universal monarch,
> we will become the humblest of servants in saṃsāra.

And (verse 74):

Know that even Brahmā himself,
after achieving happiness free from attachment,
in his turn will endure ceaseless suffering
as fuel for the fires of Avīci.[57]

THE DISTRESS OF LACKING COMPANIONS

When we die, we must go on to the next world alone. Having left behind our home, body, possessions, friends, and relatives, we will be all alone when we are pursued by the fierce winds of karma. As the same text (verse 76) says:

All alone, you will be plunged into infinite darkness
that can't be overpowered by light of sun or moon.

Śāntideva's *Introduction to the Bodhisattva's Way of Life* (2:61) says:

Just as I must eventually forsake this life,
so too must I take leave of relatives and friends.
When I must go alone on death's uncertain journey,
what concern to me are all these enemies and allies?

Reflecting on the eight sufferings

A sūtra says:

Alas, birth is suffering; old age is suffering; sickness is suffering; death is suffering; encountering the unpleasant is suffering; separation from the pleasant is suffering; seeking but not finding what we desire is suffering. In short, these five perpetuating aggregates are suffering.

1. THE SUFFERING OF BIRTH

While remaining in the womb,[58] and then when taking birth, we experience all kinds of suffering due to our mother's diet and actions, for example. We can experience intense heat, as if molten copper were being poured over our body; or intense cold, as if we were being covered in snow; or we can feel crushed, as if we were being squeezed between rocks; and we can feel our body scraped, as if we had fallen into a thorny bush. Even imagining these clearly can be a cause of unbearable suffering. Birth is also the basis and support for all future suffering.

2. THE SUFFERING OF AGING

As youth fades, our hair turns as white as mugwort,[59] our waist becomes bent over like a bow, and our skin becomes wrinkled like knotted sinews. As our strength deteriorates, we become as heavy as a sack of earth and as decrepit as an old tree, and we start to stoop and crawl like an infant. As our senses fail, we can no longer see forms as large as mountains or hear sounds as loud as trumpets, and we are unsure whether it is day or night. What is more, we can no longer dress ourselves properly nor digest our food. We are ridiculed by friends and enemies alike, and death is closing in on us.

3. THE SUFFERING OF SICKNESS

When our bodies are afflicted by a predominance of heat, cold, wind, bile, or phlegm, most food and drink causes us discomfort, and whatever we do only compounds our misery. Nothing seems pleasurable, and even if something does tempt us a little, we are too weak to enjoy it. We lose weight, our skin dries up, our joints become rigid and inflexible, and through the intervention of demonic and harmful influences, our minds become disturbed and driven crazy. To be cured, we must undergo the trials of bloodletting and cautery and take bitter-tasting medicine.

4. THE SUFFERING OF DEATH

As explained in the contemplation on impermanence, at the time of death, when the lifespan determined by our karma is exhausted, we must suffer the great agony of dying. All kinds of indications of our impending death appear to us, and we are caught by Yama's terrifying henchmen. Beloved friends and family, our home, body, and possessions must all be left behind. And, as this happens, we have no refuge or protector, no friend or ally. There is no option but to meet this terrifying destiny all alone.

5. THE SUFFERING OF ENCOUNTERING WHAT IS UNPLEASANT

Both physically and mentally, we suffer greatly through encountering—or merely dreading an encounter with—our enemies, harmful influences, precipices, fires, floods, disease, hunger, thirst, and so on in this life, and the bardos and lower realms in future existences.

6. THE SUFFERING OF SEPARATION FROM THE PLEASANT

We suffer from being separated—or even from the fear of being separated—whether temporarily or permanently, from the things we enjoy and the people we love.

7. THE SUFFERING OF SEEKING BUT NOT FINDING THE OBJECTS OF OUR DESIRES

On those occasions when we put our energy into pursuing the objects of our desires and yet fail in our pursuit, we suffer the frustration of our hopes.

8. THE SUFFERING OF THE FIVE PERPETUATING AGGREGATES

The five tainted perpetuating aggregates, by the mere fact of their existence, are suffering. Their cause is tainted, because they are produced by previous karma and destructive emotions. By their nature, they are tainted entities. And their result is also tainted, because they perpetuate similar versions of themselves. Thus they are not beyond the suffering of conditioning. It is their character, just as heat is the nature of fire or foulness is the nature of excrement. This is why the Lord of Sages perfectly declared in his teaching on the four seals: "All that is tainted is suffering."[60]

THE PARTICULAR SUFFERINGS EXPERIENCED BY BEINGS OF THE SIX REALMS

The sufferings of the gods

The gods of the form and formless realms, who are propelled by nontransferable karma, experience the bliss of samādhi and do not undergo blatant suffering upon suffering. Yet they have not gone beyond the nature of suffering entirely. They are still bound by the ties of self-grasping and under the power of karma and destructive emotions. Without any power over birth and death, they will eventually fall into the lower realms. Since they lack control over their own destiny, they are likened to a bird flying in the sky or an arrow shot into the air.

As it says in Vasubandhu's *Advice for the Assembly*:

> The gods of the form and formless realms
> are beyond the suffering of suffering,
> and they enjoy the bliss of samādhi,
> remaining for an eon without moving.
> Still this is not definitive freedom,
> and they will again be made to fall.
> It appears as if they have gone beyond
> the turbulent sufferings of lower realms,
> but try as they might, they cannot stay long.
> Like a bird flying through the sky
> or an arrow shot with childlike strength,
> they will return to earth once more.
> Like lamps that might remain alight
> but cease with each passing moment,
> they are afflicted by the sufferings
> of "changing composite things."

The gods of the desire realm too, who are propelled by their meritorious karma, still fight, threaten, intimidate, and overpower one another. Some quarrel with the demigods and are injured, maimed, and killed. All of them, when they see the signs foretelling death, and when they experience dying and transmigration, undergo greater mental suffering than those in the lower realms. As *Letter to a Friend* (verse 98) tells us:

> Although the gods of the higher realms enjoy great bliss,
> the pain they undergo at death and transmigration is greater still.

When they reflect on this, the noble minded
will not crave these terminable higher states.

You might wonder what these signs of impending death might be. The
same text (verse 99) tells us:

The body takes on an unattractive hue,
seats become uncomfortable, and flower garlands fade,
clothes develop an unpleasant odor,
and for the very first time, the body perspires.

Having died, most of these gods fall to the lower realms. The same text
(verse 101) says:

When migrating from the world of gods,
if they have no trace of virtue left,
helpless, they descend to the animals or pretas
or to the hells—whichever is befitting.

The suffering of the asuras

In addition to the sufferings already mentioned, the asuras, through
their habituation to jealousy, are tormented with feelings of hostility
brought on by the wealth and splendor enjoyed by the gods. Although
asuras have the intelligence to distinguish good from bad, they are
obscured by the ripening of past karma, which means that their physical
existence is not a suitable basis for seeing the truth, and they too will fall
once again into the lower realms. This is therefore described as a lowly
existence. *Letter to a Friend* (verse 102) says:

The asuras too suffer greatly in their minds,
naturally hostile to the riches of the gods.
Although they possess intelligence,
their obscurations prevent them from seeing the truth.

The sufferings of human beings

In addition to the sufferings of birth, old age, sickness, and death and so on, which have already been explained, human beings are always subject to pains similar to those of the lower realms, such as poverty, quarreling, panic, stress, fatigue, execution, and expulsion, relentless as the flow of a river. As Vasubandhu's *Advice for the Assembly* says:

> All the sufferings of the lower realms
> are also to be found among human beings:
> Assailed by suffering as in the hells,
> in poverty, they suffer as in the Yama world.[61]
> And the sufferings of animals too
> are present whenever the strong use
> violence and abuse the weak.
> And all continue unabated, like a river.

Āryadeva's *Four Hundred Verses* (2:8):

> The privileged suffer mentally,
> the lowly have physical pain.
> Thus suffering engulfs the world,
> oppressing us all day by day.

Although we might insist that we experience a little happiness now and then, this is just a result of our tendency to cling to suffering as happiness. In the end, everything is destined for destruction and separation, since we are not beyond the nature of suffering. As *Letter to a Friend* (verse 48ab) says:

> In truth, you must know, human beings are not happy,
> and they are impermanent, devoid of self and impure.

It also (verse 56) says:

> In the end, the body turns to ashes, dried out or putrefied.
> It becomes a thing impure, lacking any essence.

It is destroyed, worn away and decayed.
Its character, you should know, is to fall apart.

The sufferings of animals

Animals who dwell deep within the ocean and in the dark spaces between the continents are subject to fear and overwhelmed by suffering and harmful actions, such as killing and preying upon one another, from the very moment they are born. They are shrouded in the darkness of delusion, confused as to what should be adopted or avoided. Lacking the good fortune even to hear the name of the Dharma, they are cut off from all forms of happiness and good. And from darkness they fall yet further into darkness.

Animals who live scattered on the earth's surface suffer from being trapped,[62] confused,[63] ensnared in nets, killed, beaten, and enslaved for the sake of their flesh, skin, horns, bones, wool, pearls, musk, bile, and so on. They too are not beyond suffering and harmful actions. *Letter to a Friend* (verses 89–90) says:

> Animals also face all manner of suffering,
> such as being slaughtered, tied up, or beaten.
> And those who renounce virtues that bring peace
> suffer the unbearable fate of devouring one another.
>
> Some are killed for the sake of pearls or wool,
> or else for the sake of their bones, meat, or skin,
> while others, being powerless, are enslaved
> and then beaten, prodded, and whipped.

The forms and lifespan of the various animals are not uniform. The largest, such as the great sea-monsters Nyami and Demi, could be mistaken for mountains, they are so large, and even when they swallow many thousands of tiny creatures, still they are not satisfied, yet they amass a heavy burden of suffering and harmful deeds. As for their lifespan, the *Treasury of Abhidharma* (3:83) says:

The longest living animals remain for an eon.

The suffering of the pretas

The pretas who dwell in the depths live more than five hundred *yoja-nas*[64] beneath our world of Jambudvīpa and are of thirty-two kinds, the sutras explain. Those who are scattered on the surface derive from them. Their sufferings, when grouped together, are of three kinds.

1. Those with *outer obscurations* are plagued with hunger and thirst and wander far and wide in search of food and drink. When they approach the shores of lakes, pools, rivers, or wells and so on, they are confronted by guards with swords and spears and other powerful weapons, who obstruct and chase after them. Even if they reach the water, they perceive it as pus and blood or as hot ashes and are thus unable to enjoy it.

2. Those with *inner obscurations* do find food and drink but cannot fit anything inside their mouths, which are no bigger than the eye of a needle. They cannot gulp anything down their tiny throats, which are like the stalk of a lotus flower. They cannot fill their stomachs, which are as huge as mountains. And their tiny arms and legs, which are like blades of grass, are not strong enough to carry them.

3. Unable to enjoy anything pleasant, those with the *obscurations of hunger and thirst* are compelled to consume unpleasant and foul-smelling substances like excrement, urine, and mucus. Some even cut off their own flesh to eat. But whatever they consume transforms into lumps of iron and the like as soon as it enters their stomachs, burning and slicing through all their internal organs and causing them untold distress.

In short, from the very moment they are born, these creatures are tormented by hunger and thirst, their flesh and skin dry up, and their hair and nails grow long. They look like stumps of wood burnt in a fire. Deprived of anything enjoyable, they are tormented by craving and desire. The Dharma is completely unknown to them, and they are constantly tormented by heat and cold, by exhaustion and fear. *Letter to a Friend* (verses 91–95) says:

> Pretas too, who are starved of what they wish for,
> face an unbearable and unending stream of suffering

brought about by hunger, thirst, cold, heat, and fear.
Their plight is extremely difficult to endure.

Some, with mouths like the eye of a needle
and bellies like a mountain, are tortured by hunger,
and yet they do not have the power to eat
even the tiniest lump of discarded filth.

Some, who are just skin and bones, and naked,
are like the withered tops of palm trees;
while some spit flames during the night
and eat the blazing sand that falls into their mouths.

Some of the more wretched types cannot find even filth,
such as pus, or excrement, or blood, and the like,
and strike each other's faces before gobbling down the pus
that drips out from the goiters on their necks.

For pretas, even the moon seems hot in summer,
and the sun itself seems cold in wintertime;
trees and plants lose their fruits and rivers dry up
whenever they so much as glance in their direction.

The appearance of their bodies and the duration of their lives is not
fixed, but speaking generally of those whose lives are longest, the same
text (verse 96) says:

Some have their bodies tightly bound
by the noose of karma from past misdeeds
and experience sufferings without interruption.
For five or ten thousand years, they will not die.

The sufferings of the hell beings

There are three sections here: the hot hells, the cold hells, and the
ephemeral and neighboring hells.

THE HOT HELLS

The *Treasury of Abhidharma* (3:58bc–59a) says:

> Twenty thousand *yojanas* beneath the earth
> is the hell of Unrelenting Pain
> and above it, the seven other hells.

As this indicates, the eight hot hells, beginning with Unrelenting Pain (Skt. *Avīci*), lie beneath the earth, one on top of the other.

1. The Reviving Hell
Through the power of their karma associated with anger, all that the natives of this hell take hold of turns into weapons, with which they strike each other, cutting off their flesh. Whenever they lose consciousness, a voice from the sky declares: "Revive!" and they get up again and strike one another as before. The sufferings they experience defy the imagination.

2. The Black-Line Hell
The inhabitants of this hell have black lines drawn on their bodies—eight lines, or sixteen lines, and so on—by infernal guardians. Then their bodies are sliced and cut apart along these lines by blazing weapons, such as saws and axes.

3. The Crushing Hell
The inhabitants of this hell are chased by the infernal guardians between mountains shaped like iron horns or valleys resembling the heads of rams, where they are crushed again and again, causing their blood to come streaming out.

4. The Howling Hell
The inhabitants of this hell must stand upon a ground of burning iron, and when they can no longer bear it and search for a place of refuge, they see an iron house. Yet as soon as they enter it, it bursts into flames and burns both inside and out, causing them to let out wails of suffering and despair.

5. The Great Howling Hell

The inhabitants of this hell enter iron houses with double walls, and their suffering is twice as intense as that of the inhabitants of the previous hell.

6. The Heating Hell

The inhabitants of this hell are impaled on blazing iron spikes, which enter through the soles of their feet and pierce the tops of their skulls, so that flames and plumes of smoke shoot out from their orifices and all the pores of their bodies. What is more, they are plunged into iron cauldrons filled with boiling copper; or else, whenever they lie down upon the burning ground, they are pounded and chopped apart with blazing iron hammers.

7. The Intensely Heating Hell

The inhabitants of this hell are impaled on tridents, which enter through the soles of their feet and pierce through their two shoulders and the tops of their heads. The bodies, which are the basis of their suffering, the cause, which is their karma, and the essence of the suffering itself are all more intense than in the previous hell.

8. The Hell of Unrelenting Pain

The inhabitants of this hell suffer as their bodies are burned continuously by ravaging fires that blaze from every direction. It is only by the sounds of their screams that they can be recognized as sentient beings. They are plunged into the blazing fires, supine or upside down, by infernal guardians, and their tongues are pulled out and stretched with burning pincers then plowed like a field with burning iron plows, and as their skin is flayed off, they are bound with burning strips of copper, beaten with burning hammers while being verbally abused, and so on. Without even a moment's interruption, they experience sufferings that simply defy the imagination.

These hells are described in detail in the *Sūtra of the Application of Mindfulness* and in the Abhidharma texts, but *Letter to a Friend* (verses 77–79) summarizes these descriptions by saying:

For beings who act in harmful ways,
there'll be constant suffering in the hells,
including the Reviving, Black Line, Intensely Heating,
Crushing, Howling, and Unrelenting Pain.

Some are squeezed and pressed like sesame,
others ground to powder like finest flour.
Some are cut apart with saws, and others
hacked with razor-sharp axes, impossible to bear.

Likewise, some are forced to swallow
scorching drafts of molten bronze.

And (verse 82):

Some are burned in heaps of blazing coals
relentlessly, their mouths just gaping open;
and some are boiled in cauldrons made of iron,
cooked like rice dumplings, and upside down.

And (verse 85):

Of all pleasures, the exhaustion of craving
is considered to be the very highest bliss.
Likewise, of all sufferings, the pains of the hell
of unrelenting pain are the most unbearable.

As for the *duration* of these sufferings, generally it is not possible to die
and transmigrate until one's karma is exhausted. As the same text (verse
87) says:

These sufferings, so extremely difficult to bear,
are experienced for hundreds of millions of years,
and until the unwholesome karma is expended,
you'll never be parted from your life in hell.

And regarding the particular lifespans involved, the *Treasury of Abhidharma* (3:79–80) says:

> Fifty years for a human being
> is one day for the lowest of
> the gods of the desire realm,
> and they live five hundred years.
> It doubles for each of those above.

And (3:82b–83a):

> For the six hells of Reviving and the rest,
> one day and night lasts a desire god's lifetime.
> Then the number of years they live
> is similar to gods in the realm of desire.

THE COLD HELLS

The *Treasury of Abhidharma* (3:60b) says:

> The eight cold hells, such as the hell of blisters...

Directly to the north of the eight hot hells, it is said, are to be found the eight cold hells, one above the other.

In the first of these, the Hell of Blisters, inhabitants are lashed by freezing cold winds, in hollows of snow, and their skin breaks out in blisters.

In the second, the Hell of Burst Blisters, the inhabitants are lashed even harder by the freezing winds, and their blisters burst open, oozing pus.

In the third, the Hell of Chattering Teeth, the extreme cold causes the inhabitants' teeth to chatter.

In the fourth, the Hell of Lamentations, the inhabitants are so worn down with suffering that they let out piercing cries of lamentation and despair.

In the fifth, the Hell of Groans, the inhabitants are afflicted with such great suffering that they cannot manage to let out anything but the weakest of groans signaling their anguish.

In the sixth, the Hell of Utpala-Like Cracks, the freezing cold wind causes the inhabitants' skin to turn blue and to crack into five or six pieces.

In the seventh, the Hell of Lotus-Like Cracks, the inhabitants' skin turns red and splits into as many as ten pieces.

In the eighth, the Hell of Great Lotus-Like Cracks, the inhabitants' skin turns deepest red and splits open into a hundred or more pieces.

Regarding the lifespan of beings in these hells, the *Treasury of Abhidharma* (3:84b–85a) says:

> If, every hundred years, a single sesame seed were taken
> from a jar of sesame seeds, the time taken to empty the jar
> would equal the span of life in the Hell of Blisters.
> The lifespan for the rest increases twentyfold each time.

When this says "a jar of sesame seeds," this is referring to a container capable of holding eighty Magadhan measures[65] filled to the brim with sesame seeds. If a single seed were taken from such a vase once every hundred years, the time taken to empty the whole vase would equal the span of life in the Hell of Blisters. Then, for each of the hells below this, the lifespan increases by a factor of twenty each time.

THE EPHEMERAL AND NEIGHBORING HELLS

The *ephemeral hells* are located near the main hot and cold hells and on the shores of the ocean and in other places, as described in the accounts of Saṅgharakṣita.[66]

The *neighboring hells* are described as follows in the *Treasury of Abhidharma* (3:59b–60a):

> For all eight, there are sixteen remaining hells:
> the Pit of Burning Embers and Swamp of Putrefying Corpses,
> the Road of Razor Blades and so on, and the Unfordable River.

These four neighboring hells are located around the hot hells.

1. In the *Pit of Burning Embers* beings sink down to their knees, and all their flesh and skin is burned from their legs, so that only the bones remain. Then, each time they lift their legs, the flesh grows back.

2. Outside this, there lies the *Swamp of Putrefying Corpses*, which emits a foul stench like raw sewage and burns intensely like fire. As beings fall into it, they are eaten from head to toe by worms with iron beaks called "razor-beaked swamp worms."

3. Farther out there is the *Road of Razor Blades* and so on. As beings pass through the plain filled with razor blades, when they put down their feet and lift them up again, the flesh is stripped away and then restored. Situated nearby is the *Forest of Sword Blades*, in which the trees have burning iron swords for leaves, cutting and stabbing the limbs and vital organs of the hell beings who wander inside. When beings flee and fall inside, they are attacked and eaten by terrifying dogs with iron jaws. Next to this are the *shalmali* trees, which are trees made of iron with a great many thorns, each sixteen finger-widths in size. When beings are impelled by their karma to climb these trees, the thorns all point downward, and when the beings descend, the thorns turn around and point upward, so that their flesh and skin are all cut open and flayed off. Ravens with metallic beaks and claws land on their heads and shoulders and pluck out their eyes and tongue. Since these all involve injury through weapons, they are counted as a single location.

4. The *Unfordable River*. Sinking in boiling caustic water and then floating back to the surface, their flesh and skin are burned and then restored. Whenever they escape to its shores, Yama's minions scold them and harm them in various ways.

These four are located around each of the eight hot hells. Since they are found in each of the four directions, there are sixteen altogether.

In the same vein, *Letter to a Friend* (verse 71) says:

> But consider, if you will, the unbearable suffering
> of wading through burning embers and rotten corpses.

And (verse 70):

Then you'll have to endure the unbearable sensation
of hells' crushing, cutting, and tearing devices.

And (verse 72):

Then you'll arrive at groves whose sword-like leaves
cut off your arms and legs, your ears and nose.

And (verses 79–80):

And some are impaled on stakes
of barbed and fiercely burning iron.

Some, whom ferocious dogs with iron fangs
will rip to shreds, throw up their hands,
and others, powerless, are pecked by ravens,
with sharp metallic beaks and terrible claws.

As well as (verse 73):

Then you'll be plunged into the Unfordable River,
with its intolerably caustic boiling waters.

Wherever we are born in these hells just described, we will experience
sufferings beyond measure. As the same text (verse 86) says:

You might be stabbed here for one whole day,
violently, with three hundred spears,
but that wouldn't approximate or match
a portion of even the tiniest sufferings in hell.

And (verse 84):

And if just seeing pictures of the hells, or hearing,
reading, and thinking about them brings such terror,

what will you do when you experience there
the unbearable effects of your past actions?

This being so, when it is only the ceasing of our breath that separates
us from this place of rebirth, merely hearing of which strikes terror in
our hearts, a person who remains without a care can only be bereft of
genuine feeling. As the same text (verse 83) says:

The ceasing of his breath is all that separates
an evildoer from hell's boundless suffering.
Anyone who hears this yet remains unmoved
must have a mind as hard as a diamond.

In conclusion, all three realms of saṃsāric existence are like a pit of
fire, because we are continually afflicted with different forms of suffering, difficult even to contemplate. They are like a plain of razors,
because our body and mind are inflicted with pain of many kinds. They
are like a pit of filth, because they are always polluted with the debris
of karma and destructive emotions. They are like a slaughterhouse,
because they are terrifying and difficult to escape from. As the same
text (verse 103) says:

Know that saṃsāra is like this: we are reborn
as gods, humans, hell beings, pretas, or animals,
but such birth is not good;
in fact, it has countless ills in store.

Therefore, those who possess the intelligence to distinguish good from
bad will set aside all forms of meaningless activity and strive continuously to apply the methods for liberating themselves and others from
this infinite ocean of suffering, since nothing could be more important.
With this point in mind, the glorious Nāgārjuna also said (verse 104):

Even if your hair or clothing should suddenly catch fire,
rather than expending your energy trying to avert it,

direct your effort toward preventing future rebirth,
knowing that nothing could be of greater importance.

Unless we contemplate the trials of saṃsāra in detail like this, there will be no opportunity for us to develop the wish for liberation or great compassion. That is why we must contemplate again and again, and make a firm decision to follow the path to liberation. Knowing that the most important factor on this path is precious bodhicitta, we will do whatever we can to make it arise, sustain it, and make it increase.

In order to clothe ourselves in this great armor and develop our mindfulness and awareness, we can recite aloud the following quotations and others like them and contemplate their meaning.

The *Sūtra of the Application of Mindfulness* says:

> Beings in hell are plagued by its infernal fires,
> pretas are plagued by hunger and thirst,
> animals are plagued by preying on one another,
> the gods are plagued by their lack of care,
> human beings are plagued by their short lives—
> in saṃsāra, there is never even the slightest joy,
> not even so much as a needle tip's worth.

And Maitreya's *Sublime Continuum* (4:50) says:

> In saṃsāra's beginningless cycle of birth and death, there are five
> different courses beings can take.
> Just as there can be no pleasant fragrance in a cesspit, there is no
> joy among these five classes of beings.

꘎

Blazing with unbearable suffering, like a pit of flames,
polluted by all manner of impurities, like a pool of filth,
difficult to cross, this infinite ocean of existence—
turn your minds from this, all you who seek liberation!

CONCLUSION

When we train our minds thoroughly in these preliminaries and then take pains accordingly to adopt and avoid certain courses of action, this encompasses all the points of practice necessary for the beings of lesser and intermediate capacity, as they are explained in the *Lamp for the Path to Enlightenment* and elsewhere. To fear the sufferings of the lower realms, and then to adopt or avoid actions for the sake of gaining the happiness of the higher realms alone, is the approach of beings of lesser capacity. To regard the whole of samsāra as a mass of fire, and to strive on the path of liberation in order to free oneself alone is the approach of beings of intermediate capacity. As Atiśa's *Lamp for the Path to Enlightenment* (verses 3–4) says:

Those who strive by any means
to gain only the pleasures of samsāra
for themselves alone—
such people are called "lesser" individuals.

Those who turn their backs on worldly pleasures,
and avoid any harmful actions,
striving for peace for themselves alone—
such individuals are said to be "intermediate."

Then, by considering how unbearable it would be for these sufferings of saṃsāra—which I have here described—to befall us, the wish that the sufferings of all limitless beings might be eliminated and the meditation on the two kinds of bodhicitta directed toward that goal is the approach of beings of greater spiritual capacity. As the same text (verse 5) says:

> Those who long to put a complete end
> to all the sufferings of others
> through the sufferings of their own experience—
> individuals such as these are supreme.

If we understand this, we can see that these instructions include all the most essential themes of the gradual path of the three types of individual. This is certainly the kind of infallible approach taken by glorious Atiśa: leading the majority of students along the gradual paths of the three types of individual and guiding only a few supreme students using the instructions on mind training.

7. Relative Bodhicitta: The Holy Secret

The main practice is divided into two parts: training in relative bodhicitta, and training in absolute bodhicitta.

From the root text:

Once stability is reached, teach the secret.

This means that once stability in relative bodhicitta has been reached, then absolute bodhicitta, which is kept secret from those not yet ready to receive it, can be taught. It therefore shows the proper sequence of these two.

This line does not appear in some texts, and some teachers of the past would begin with the meditation on absolute bodhicitta. Of course, this way of doing things is not significantly different, but it is slightly inappropriate—firstly because this line does appear in several texts of pure origin, and secondly because it goes against the sequence of the general teachings on the path, which present the standard order of relative and absolute, means and wisdom, or merit and wisdom, and also the sequence of the three trainings,[67] the six perfections,[68] and so on.

So let us begin with the cultivation of relative bodhicitta. This is divided into two: practice during the session and practice between sessions.

PRACTICE DURING THE SESSION

Train in the two—giving and taking—alternately.
These two are to be mounted on the breath.

In the general scriptural tradition of the Mahāyāna, there is the meditation of the "seven-stage training in cause and effect," but here, rather like straightening a tree that has grown crooked,[69] the approach is to cultivate the bodhicitta of exchanging oneself for others from the very beginning.[70] This is not a practice for those of lesser mental capacity, as it is powerful mind training and a most marvelous feature of the Mahāyāna. Śāntideva's *Introduction to the Way of the Bodhisattva* (8:120) says:

> Whoever wishes to afford protection
> quickly to both himself and others
> should practice that most holy secret:
> the exchanging of oneself for others.

Similarly, in Sakya Paṇḍita's *Clear Differentiation of the Three Sets of Vows* (2:44), it says:

> The exchange of oneself for others is said
> to be the heart of Buddha's teachings.

And then, more elaborately (2:50):

> Therefore this exchange of oneself for others
> leads swiftly to complete enlightenment
> and, even before then, it is said,
> is a source of all the bounties of this world.

Without relying on this method, we cannot secure either temporary or ultimate happiness and well-being. *Introduction to the Way of the Bodhisattva* (8:131) tells us:

Unless I can give away my happiness
in exchange for others' suffering,
I will not attain the awakening I seek,
and even in saṃsāra I'll find no joy.

Clear Differentiation of the Three Sets of Vows (2:51) says:

But if one errs in the key points of bodhicitta,
enlightenment will not be gained through any other teaching.

There are three sections: the practice of taking, the practice of sending, and the practice of alternating.

The practice of taking

This has two parts: the logic of the practice and the stages of the practice.

THE LOGIC OF THE PRACTICE

It is logical that the enemy, the source of all the problems in the world, self-cherishing, should be destroyed using a powerful antidote. In the *Jātakas* it is said:

Alas! To cherish only oneself
is utterly inappropriate and unbearable.

And:

This enemy, the attitude of self-cherishing—
who would seek to enhance it?

If we do not do this practice, and instead we remain attached to ourselves while feeling aversion to others, there will be no way for us to relinquish our burden of suffering and negative deeds. As it says in Maitreya's *Ornament of Mahāyāna Sūtras* (chapter 6):

Foolish beings exert themselves for the sake of their own happiness,
but never finding it, they experience only suffering.

Dharmakīrti's *Commentary on Valid Cognition* (2:221) says:

When there is an "I," there is a perception of other,
and from the ideas of self and other come attachment and
      aversion;
as a result of getting wrapped up in these,
all possible faults come into being.

Introduction to the Bodhisattva's Way of Life (8:134) says:

If all the harm within the world
and all the fears and sufferings
derive only from clinging to a self,
what need have I for such a demon?

And (8:154):

This is the one who, hundreds of times
in cyclic existence, has done me harm.

THE STAGES OF THE PRACTICE

In this there are three parts: meditation on love, meditation on taking
by means of compassion, and meditation on bodhicitta.

Meditation on love

In general, as it says in the *Ornament of Mahāyāna Sūtras* (17:17):

The bodhisattvas have abandoned factors incompatible with the
      four immeasurables,[71]
are endowed with the wisdom that is nonconceptual,
engage with the three objects of focus,
and bring beings to full maturity.

For love and the other immeasurables, the text says, there are four special features:

1. The special feature of the *absent* is the relinquishing of the particular discordant factors.
2. The special feature of the *supporting factor* is the presence of nonconceptual wisdom.
3. The special feature of the *objects of focus* is the direction toward the three kinds of objects, namely sentient beings, phenomena, and the nonreferential.
4. The special feature of the *function* is to bring beings to full maturity.

Here, in this context, we are concerned with love that is directed toward sentient beings. Its essence is as follows: focusing on the object, sentient beings, and wishing that they may have happiness and its causes, namely virtuous actions.

Candrakīrti's *Introduction to the Middle Way* (6:211) says:

And great loving kindness is the name given
to his [i.e., the Buddha's] activity for benefiting beings.

Since it is easier for love to arise if we begin the practice by focusing on our mother from this present life, we visualize our mother in front of us and bring to mind the ways in which she has shown us great kindness. We think:

From the time I was in her womb, she did all that she could and used all the means at her disposal in order to benefit me and save me from harm. Fearing that I might fall sick or die, she worked tirelessly to serve me and nurse me back to health. She held me in her love and looked at me with affection. She chewed my food for me before putting it in my mouth. She wiped me clean with her hands and warmed me with the heat of her own body. She called me by affectionate names. Rather than taking food or clothing for herself, or using whatever wealth she had for her own enjoyment, she gave it all to me. She taught me the means to communicate and how to act and all the skills I needed. In short, she bore all kinds of hardship and tribulation for my sake.

Think about this carefully and generate a feeling of intense closeness and affection.

When you have generated this feeling, consider that it is not just in this present lifetime but again and again throughout beginningless time that she has looked after you with such kindness. As it says in the sūtras:

> All the breast milk that we drank
> when each sentient being was our mother
> is greater in volume than all the water
> contained within the four great oceans.

This is how we remember the kindness of our mothers.

Then we consider how this kind mother of ours lacks happiness and its causes, which are positive actions. We think:

> Now my mother has gained a human body with all the freedoms and advantages, but she does not have the capacity to realize its full potential. She lacks the discernment to tell right from wrong, and her virtuous intentions and actions are weak, naturally drawing her into unwholesome ways. Since it will therefore be difficult for her to experience even the happiness of the higher realms, what need is there to mention the bliss of liberation and omniscience?

When you feel certain about this, think to yourself, "May my mother come to possess abundant happiness and the virtues that are its causes! In order for this to happen, she must be freed from the adverse conditions that prevent it, so may the burden of all her suffering and harmful acts ripen on me!" Pray like this from the depths of your heart, and recite the words aloud. At the same time, consider that all your mother's harmful actions and suffering take the form of black smoke,[72] which you draw into your heart. Meditate on this with great joy.

When you gain some proficiency in this, focus on your father and other close relations and friends, and consider the kindness they have shown you in this and previous lives, as before. Then extend the practice to those who are neutral, meaning they are neither friend nor foe, and then to your enemies, both human and nonhuman. Think:

> All these beings have been my father and mother again and again throughout beginningless time, and at that time they treated me with just as much kindness as my current mother and father. Now that we have passed on into further lives, I no longer recognize them, and so I feel attachment to some and aversion to others, but that is simply the result of my delusion. How wonderful it would be if all these beings—all equal in terms of their kindness—could find happiness!

Continue the stages of the practice just as before. Then extend the focus of your practice even further and consider all the beings of a single continent, and then all four continents, then this cosmos of a billion worlds, and finally the whole infinity of beings, as boundless as space itself.

Kamalaśīla's *Stages of Meditation II* expresses this eloquently in the following way:

> Consider how all sentient beings want happiness and how they do not want suffering. In the course of our beginningless wanderings throughout existence, there is not a single sentient being who has not been our close relation hundreds of times, so why do we treat them differently, feeling desire and attachment toward some and anger toward others? We should begin the meditation on love by considering our close friends and relations and wishing that they find happiness.

Then we must gradually extend the practice to ordinary people and even enemies.

Concerning the benefits of meditating on love in this way, the *King of Samādhi Sūtra* says:

> Even an offering throughout billions of realms
> consisting of gifts infinite in number and variety
> presented to great beings every day for all eternity
> could not match the wonder of a mind of love.

Nāgārjuna's *Precious Garland* (2:83–85) says:

> Offerings of three hundred pots of food
> made three times each and every day
> could not match even a portion of the merit
> gained from just a single moment's loving kindness.

> Even if it does not bring you liberation,
> it will produce the eight rewards of love:
> Gods and humans will care for you,
> and they will offer you protection;

> You will be happy and know many joys;
> no poison or weapon will do you harm;
> effortlessly, you will achieve your aims;
> and you will be born in Brahmā's realm.

Moreover, as the lamas of the past would say:

> The accounts of Daughter and so on[73]
> provide the background to this instruction.

We must therefore study and recollect such stories.

Like water rinsing away the stains of past misdeeds,
this method for extinguishing the flames of hatred
and providing conditions for compassion's magic tree to grow—
a mind of loving kindness, may it saturate my being!

Meditation on taking by means of compassion
Compassion arises easily once we possess the kind of love that has been described, so next we meditate on compassion. *Stages of Meditation II* says:

> When a person's mind is saturated with love, like ground that has been moistened, the seed of compassion, once planted, will easily grow. Thus, having permeated the mind with love, cultivate compassion.

The essence of compassion is as follows: It is directed toward beings who possess suffering and its causes and is the wish that they might be freed from this suffering. The same text says:

> Compassion is the wish that those who have suffering may be freed from it.

This is the root of the Mahāyāna path and the principal cause of omniscience. It is crucial in the beginning, middle, and end. The *Compendium of Dharma Sūtra*:

> O Bhagavan, a bodhisattva should not train in many practices. O Bhagavan, if a bodhisattva keeps to a single practice and learns it perfectly, he has all the Buddha's teachings in

the palm of his hand. What is that single practice? It is great
compassion.

And Candrakīrti's *Introduction to the Middle Way* (1:2) says:

> Love is the seed of this abundant harvest of buddhahood.
> It is like the water that causes growth and expansion,
> and it ripens into the state of lasting enjoyment.
> Therefore, at the outset, I praise compassion!

Visualize, in the space before you, your mother from the present life,
and consider in detail all her acts of great kindness. As repayment for
this great kindness, she must be benefited and protected from any harm.
When you examine what is beneficial and what is harmful, you can see
with complete certainty that happiness and virtue are beneficial for
her, while suffering and negative actions are harmful. Yet this mother
of yours lacks happiness and its causes and is oppressed by suffering and
its causes. As *Introduction to the Bodhisattva's Way of Life* (1:28) says:

> Although seeking to avoid pain,
> they run headlong into suffering.
> Though longing for happiness, they foolishly
> destroy it, as if it were an enemy.

Therefore, just as in the contemplation on the faults of saṃsāra, consider the suffering and causes of suffering within your mother's mind-
stream, and reflect again and again on how vast and powerful they are.
When the contemplation becomes overpowering, and you feel the hairs
of your body standing on end, your flesh shivering, and tears streaming
from your eyes, say to yourself: "How I wish that my mother were free
from all these sufferings and their causes! May she be free! I shall be the
one to free her! I pray to the teacher and the Three Jewels that she may
be free." Say these words aloud and meditate on them from the depths
of your heart.

If you practice like this but still do not develop compassion, then take yourself to an isolated, expansive place. Sit yourself down in a posture of despair and reproach yourself, declaring your own faults until you feel ashamed and full of regret. Say to yourself:

> Alas! I am poor in fortune and meager are my merits. I have only weak potential and capacity for the Mahāyāna, and I am unaccustomed to the path of bodhicitta—so much so that I cannot generate compassion even for my very own mother. If this should continue, what will become of me? What will be my destiny? I will only be ashamed before the buddhas and bodhisattvas. So now I pray to you, my teacher and the Three Jewels, embodiments of inconceivable wisdom, love, and power: With your compassionate gaze, you look out for lowly beings, so look with special care upon the likes of me! Grant me your blessings, so that I may swiftly develop love, compassion, and the precious mind of bodhicitta!

Be sure to combine this with the practice of guru yoga.

Then, once again, visualize your mother before you and carefully consider all her sufferings. When you feel your heart beating suddenly, as if a spark had landed on your naked flesh, call out loudly, saying, "Mother, mother!" And, strengthening your resolve, cultivate compassion.

When you feel a deep, heartfelt wish that she may be free from suffering, take upon yourself, just as before, all her physical illness, mental anguish, negative actions of body, speech, and mind, and everything unwanted and unfavorable. Then extend the scope of the practice like before, so that in the end you have clearly imagined all limitless sentient beings, particularly those who do you harm. Reflect carefully on how they have all been your mother infinite times in the past, how they treated you with great kindness, and how they are now suffering. Consider in particular those who cause you harm: they too have been your kind mothers time and again, but now, failing to recognize this, due to their own destructive emotions as the cause and your bad karma as the contributing condition, they are acting harmfully, as if deranged and devoid of self-control, with the result that they will fall once more into the lower realms. The foremost master Tutop Wangchuk—the mahāsiddha Virūpa—said:

> These harmdoers too are my mothers.
> In the past they helped me many times,
> but as if driven mad, they lack self-control,
> and their misdeeds will bring unrelenting torment.[74]

The *Compendium of Training* says:

> Crazed by destructive emotions, blinded by delusion,
> on a treacherous pathway alongside steep ravines,
> stumbling with each and every step we take,
> I and others are always laying the foundation for future misery.
> All beings are alike in their suffering.

Generate certainty about this, and recite the following words while bringing to mind their meaning:

> *Kyemao kyihü*! My heart goes out to all these beings—my old
>   mothers—as vast in number as space itself!
> Old mothers of mine, you were my parents over and over again
>   in the past.
> At those times, you cared for me with boundless kindness,
> but not recognizing this, having passed on and been reborn,
> as if crazed, you lack freedom and self-control
> and are in the process of harming yourselves and others.
> My heart goes out to you, old mothers of mine,
> sunk in the pit of conditioned existence,
> driven mad by the demon of clinging to things as real,
> afflicted by the sickness of the destructive emotions,
> tossed to and fro in the ocean of desire,
> tormented by the flames of hatred,

enshrouded in the darkness of ignorance,
crushed under the mountain of pride,
swept up in the fierce winds of envy,
bound in the tight knots of avarice,
trapped in the net of doubt,
wandering in the forests of false belief,
propelled by the winds of evil karma,
submerged in rivers of suffering,
lost in the abyss of the lower realms,
beset by intense heat and cold,
plagued by perpetual hunger and thirst,
benighted by folly,
menaced by weapons of conflict,
worn down by craving and poverty,
stricken by signs of impending death,
led on by the messengers of Yama,
passing through the perilous pathways of the bardos,
alone and heading toward a terrifying end,
deceived by evil companions,
caught in the noose of Māra,[75] cut off from the protection and
    refuge of friends and allies,
endlessly roaming throughout saṃsāra—
old mothers of mine, my heart goes out to you all!

Say the words with feeling, and without any pretense, so that they reso-
nate deep inside you and penetrate to the core of your bones.

When, through practicing this with confident trust, you reach the
point at which you would willingly take on others' suffering, meditate
once again on the practice of taking, just as before.

These stages for meditating on great compassion are outlined very
clearly in *Stages of Meditation II*:

> Therefore, consider how all beings are immersed in the burn-
> ing flames of suffering and consider that, just like you, they
> do not wish to suffer. Say to yourself: "Alas! When all these

sentient beings, who are so dear to me, are suffering, I must free them from their pain!" Meditate so that this compassion, which is the thought of wishing others to be free from their suffering, just as if you yourself were experiencing it, extends to include all beings, not just when you are in sessions of meditation but throughout all your activities. In the beginning, at least, you can consider only your family and friends, and meditate by imagining that they experience the kinds of sufferings mentioned earlier. Next, consider all beings equally, without any partiality, and reflect that they are all your very own family and friends. Reflecting on this thoroughly, extend the meditation to include those you consider to be neutral. When you rest in meditation on compassion for family and friends, consider that you extend this feeling to all beings in all directions. When you feel spontaneous compassion, characterized by a yearning to remove pain, just like a mother seeing the suffering of her dearly beloved child, and you can extend this equally to all beings, then you can say that it has reached perfection and is fit to be called *great compassion*.

How to meditate on compassion, wishing that the suffering experienced by your chosen subjects may be pacified, is also clearly explained in several sūtras. The *Sūtra Requested by the Sovereign Lord of Dhāraṇīs*, for example, says:

> Alas! These beings, who are slaves to existence, are stained by attachment to their wives, sons, and daughters. They lack independence. Having no control, they lack genuine self-protection. Thinking, "In order that they might gain independence and self-protection and move toward happiness, I must teach them the Dharma," the bodhisattva arouses great compassion for sentient beings.
>
> Alas! These beings disagree among themselves and harbor so much anger, aggression, and malice. They lack indepen-

dence. Having no control, they lack genuine self-protection. Thinking, "In order that they might gain independence and self-protection and move toward happiness, I must teach them the Dharma," the bodhisattva arouses great compassion for sentient beings.

Alas! These beings embrace evil friends and are without any spiritual friends. They act in harmful ways. They lack independence. ...etc.

Alas! These beings are withered and overpowered by their desires, discontented, and lack the stability of the wisdom of the noble ones. They lack independence. ...etc.

Alas! These beings are blinded by their ignorance and delusion. They cling to a self, a being, a life force, a shell, a person, and an individual. They lack independence. ...etc.

Alas! These beings are caught in the noose of Māra. They remain deceitful and arrogant. They lack independence. ...etc.

Alas! These beings have closed the gateway to nirvāṇa and opened the gateway to the lower realms. They lack independence. ...etc.

The text also explains in detail how the compassion of the bodhisattvas arises toward these beings.

Therefore, rather than imitating those who seek results without first cultivating the necessary causes, we must put our effort into planting the seeds of compassion, which is the essence of the Dharma. As it is also the root of both the Mahāyāna refuge and the generation of bodhicitta and the source of all mundane and supermundane qualities, it says in the *Ornament of Mahāyāna Sūtras* (3:11):

This, the commitment made when seeking the real, is also known to come from love.[76]

And (5:3):

Its root is asserted to be compassion.

And (18:41):

> Who would not be compassionate toward beings,
> who are the source of the virtue of great compassion?

⁓ꙮ⁓

> *An ornament to beautify the mansion of great liberation,*
> *a basis for the great celebration of twofold benefit,*
> *the source of bodhicitta, this mind of compassion—*
> *be sure to cultivate it, by applying effort, all you fortunate ones!*

Meditation on taking by means of bodhicitta

It is in those who possess love, which is wishing others happiness, and compassion, which is the wish to free them from suffering, that bodhicitta, the wish to bring about their ultimate benefit, arises. Therefore, the most important practice on the path is to cultivate bodhicitta, since it is the seed of perfect buddhahood, the entranceway to the Mahāyāna, and the source of all happiness and good. As it says in the *Gaṇḍhavyūha Sūtra*:

> Son of good family, bodhicitta is like the seed of all the buddhas' qualities. It is like a field in which all the virtuous qualities of beings can grow. It is like a raging apocalyptic fire, burning away all harmful deeds. It is like a chasm in the earth, swallowing all unwholesome traits. It is like the supreme wish-fulfilling jewel, accomplishing all that could be wished for. It is like an excellent vase, perfectly providing all that we desire. It is like a hook lifting beings out of the waters of saṃsāra. It is like a sacred shrine venerated by gods, humans, and asuras. In short, whatever virtues and qualities are possessed by the buddhas, the qualities and benefits of

bodhicitta are equally extensive. Why? Because all the realms of a bodhisattvas' activity arise from it. Even the bodhisattvas of past, present, and future arise from bodhicitta.

This is how it is explained in some detail. Similarly, Bhāvaviveka's *Heart of the Middle Way* (1:1) says:

> The seed of buddhahood is bodhicitta,
> adorned with love and compassion
> and great wisdom;
> the wise therefore do not forsake it.

Regarding the essence of bodhicitta, Maitreya's *Ornament of Clear Realization* (1:18) says:

> Bodhicitta is: for the sake of others,
> longing to attain complete enlightenment.

As this says, bodhicitta is the thought of seeking the goal, which is perfect enlightenment, for the sake of the objective, which is benefiting others. There are many means of classifying bodhicitta, but since on this occasion we are concerned with relative bodhicitta, and mainly the bodhicitta of aspiration, there are three types: king-like bodhicitta, boatman-like bodhicitta, and shepherd-like bodhicitta. Of these, we are primarily concerned with the third type, because our attitude here is one of putting ourselves aside initially and wishing intensely to lead others to buddhahood. As the *Dharmasaṃgīti Sūtra* says:

> Bhagavan, the bodhisattva first awakens all beings, not himself.

As for how bodhicitta is cultivated, to pursue a state of peace for ourselves alone, while all beings—who are our very own mothers—languish in the ocean of suffering, would be quite shameless. As it says in Candragomin's *Letter to a Disciple* (verse 96):

To see our dear ones submerged in saṃsāra's ocean,
as if they had fallen into a swirling pool,
but failing to recognize them after birth and death, to then
    abandon them,
only to escape alone—what could be more shameless?

Therefore, the *Precious Garland* (5:85) says:

As long as there are beings
who still have not been freed,
for their sake, may I still remain
even after gaining unsurpassed awakening.

As this says, we must have the noble intention to be able to put aside
our own awakening for the sake of even just a single being and to take
on the burden of working for others' benefit. As it says in the *Sūtra of
the Secret of the Tathāgatas*:

"Bhagavan, who possesses bodhicitta?"
    "Your Majesty, it is possessed by whomsoever has a noble
intention that is stable and unperturbed."

There are many possible ways to bring about the goal of benefiting
others, and they could all be suitable as objectives in the right circumstances. Yet in the ultimate analysis, the higher realms do not last and
are not beyond suffering, and even the lower forms of awakening neither bring full benefit to oneself nor contribute to others' welfare. If we
were to follow these approaches, it would still be necessary to enter the
Mahāyāna eventually, and at that time any past inclinations for lesser
paths would only slow down the process of gaining realization. With
many drawbacks such as these, they are clearly not the main objective.
The principal goal therefore is nothing other than buddhahood, the
state in which the two kinds of obscuration are overcome entirely, the
two kāyas attained, and one's own and others' benefit brought about
spontaneously.

Therefore we must say to ourselves: "How wonderful it would be if all beings could attain this precious state of perfect enlightenment! They must attain it! I shall be the one to help them attain it! Through the wisdom and care of the lama and the Three Jewels, may they attain it!"

As we think in this way, we must ensure that our body, speech, and mind are in unison. Then, in order to bring this about, we meditate in different ways, repeatedly and using various methods. We say to ourselves, "May the causes of suffering present in all beings, as well as the result, which is suffering itself, and the stains of the two obscurations—in short, anything that obstructs the attainment of the higher realms, liberation, and omniscience, together with its seeds and habitual tendencies—all ripen on me!" and so on. With this, we consider that the objects of our practice are freed from every kind of fault and gain every excellence. This we should do repeatedly, counting the visualizations in the session.

Even to cultivate bodhicitta like this just once is said to produce boundless merit. As it says in the *Sūtra Requested by Viradatta*:

> If the merit of the mind of awakening
> were to take on form,
> it would fill the whole of space
> and more besides.
> A person might offer to the Lord of the World
> as many buddhafields as there are grains of sand in the Ganges,
> all filled with precious gems,
> but greater still is the offering made
> by holding one's palms together
> and mentally paying homage to bodhicitta,
> because such an act is without limit.

The text continues with other such statements and examples.

If, by contrast, we lack bodhicitta but still exert ourselves on other paths, we cannot advance beyond the extreme of quiescence. As it says in the *Ornament of Mahāyāna Sūtras* (5:21):

Those who forsake bodhicitta, which is so exceedingly worthy
    of praise,
may find quiescence but will miss out on the joys of intending
    others' benefit,
seeking methods for doing so, understanding great wisdom,
and seeing the truth of this.

Having developed some certainty about the advantages of having
bodhicitta and the faults of being without it, we must train methodi-
cally in the ways of generating bodhicitta in our own and others' minds,
causing it to remain and to increase further and further. As Lord Atiśa
said:

Those who seek to enter the doorway to the Mahāyāna teachings
must exert themselves even for an eon
to arouse this sun and moon-like bodhicitta,
which dispels the darkness and quells afflictions.

You might assume that great benefits are not to be gained merely by
the bodhicitta of aspiration, but that is incorrect. As *Introduction to the
Bodhisattva's Way of Life* (1:9) tells us:

For the very instant that bodhicitta is born
in the weary captives enslaved within saṃsāra,
they are called heirs of the bliss-gone buddhas,
honorable to gods, humans, and the world.

In this and other verses the benefits are explained in detail, mainly in
terms of the bodhicitta of aspiration. And the *Liberation of Maitreya*
describes the advantages of the bodhicitta of aspiration, which is still
lacking earnest application, with the following analogy:

Son of good family, it is like this. A diamond, even if it is
flawed, surpasses in its splendor all the most splendid jewelry
made of gold. It does not lose the name of diamond, and it can

dispel all poverty. Son of good family, in just the same way, to the omniscient mind, the diamond of bodhicitta, even if it lacks the element of earnest application, still surpasses the golden jewelry of the śrāvakas' and pratyekabuddhas' qualities. Those who possess it do not lose the name of bodhisattvas, and they can dispel all the poverty of saṃsāra.

The *Śūraṅgama Sūtra* says:

> If it is taught that even to generate bodhicitta superficially can become a cause of buddhahood, what need is there to mention carrying out various virtuous deeds and generating bodhicitta?

There are countless other such quotations.

~ ❦ ~

The ocean of compassion is unfathomable in its depth and breadth,
and in the center of noble intention's vast and stable golden expanse
is bodhicitta, finely crafted from the supreme of precious substances,
the most perfect splendor of all existence and quiescence.

Meditation on giving

This has two parts: the logic of the practice and the stages of the practice.

THE LOGIC OF THE PRACTICE

The practice of training the mind in giving is a crucial instruction—this should be understood. Why? Because we must repay the kindness all beings have shown us throughout beginningless time as well as the unimaginable karmic debt we owe them. As it says in the *Dhāraṇī of Infinite Gateways*:

Sentient beings often quarrel among themselves,
and the underlying basis of this is strong attachment.
We must therefore give away the objects of our craving.
And having given up our craving, we gain *dhāraṇī.*[77]

As this says, we must let go of the bonds of miserliness that lie at the root
of our faults. *Introduction to the Bodhisattva's Way of Life* (5:101) says:

Whether directly or even indirectly,
we must do nothing but work for others' good.

As this advises, we must apply ourselves entirely to the goal of benefiting others. The same text (3:12) also says:

By letting go of all, I will attain nirvāṇa,
the transcendence of misery I seek;
since everything must finally be abandoned,
it would be best if I gave it all away.

It is certain that we must eventually leave behind our bodies, possessions, and so on, so to give them away now, either directly or in our
imagination, is a way of making them meaningful and will also be the
cause of attaining nirvāṇa.

    Śāntideva's *Compendium of Training* says:

My body and my possessions,
and all my virtues from the past, present, and future,
I give away to all sentient beings,
and I protect, purify, and increase them.

As this says, the entire training of a bodhisattva can be summarized as
giving away, protecting, purifying, and increasing one's body, possessions, and sources of merit from the past, present, and future. The *Precious Garland* (3:12) says:

The form kāya of the buddhas
arises from stores of merit.

It is certainly our stores of merit that create the perfect environment,
body, possessions, and activity at the level of enlightenment, and here
there follows a skillful method for accomplishing now, in our imagination, the great waves of activity that are carried out in actuality by the
bodhisattvas on the bhūmis.

THE STAGES OF THE PRACTICE

This has three parts: giving away our body, giving away our possessions,
and giving away our sources of merit.

Giving away our body

For this, we transfer our mind into the heart of our yidam deity, whichever it might be, and consider that our body, which is still embraced by
the mind, grows larger, fleshier,[78] and more radiant and lustrous than
before. We then dissect it mentally, dividing it into skin, flesh, blood,
bones, internal organs, heart, limbs, and so on, all of which pervade
throughout the billionfold universe. We utter the three syllables [oṃ
āḥ hūṃ] and consider that everything is blessed and transformed into
nectar, which we then offer to the four types of guests.[79] They all receive
whatever they desire and are satisfied. We offer particularly to those
harmful influences and obstructing forces to whom we owe karmic
debts.

Giving away our possessions

For this, we bring to mind all the food and wealth we own, and all our
fields and houses and everyday possessions, and visualize them all laid
out before us. Then we bless them, so that they are transformed into
inexhaustible riches, which we offer to the four types of guests. The
offerings are transformed into billions of wish-fulfilling gems, wish-
granting trees, excellent vases, and treasuries of priceless jewels, and are
shared among all the guests, who are thereby satisfied. We offer particularly to the poor and disadvantaged.

Giving away our sources of merit

Here, we bring to mind all our sources of merit from the past, present, and future, all gathered together. Then we consider that they are blessed and transformed into an inexhaustible collection of Dharma, of both transmission and realization. By giving this to beings, we consider that the splendor and richness of Dharma increases. In particular, as it says in the *Ornament of Mahāyāna Sūtras* (4:11):

> Some commit only harmful deeds,
> some have destroyed all positive tendencies,
> some lack any virtue conducive to liberation,
> some have feeble virtue, and others lack the cause.

As this says, we give especially to those who are poor in terms of the Dharma—those who have committed the crimes with immediate retribution and so on, or who hold wrong views, or whose potential for enlightenment is only weak, or who are obscured by defects to their potential, and so on.

Furthermore, we should practice the mind training of the wish-fulfilling jewel, the mind training of the four elements, and so on according to the practical instructions of the great saints of the past, by following quotations such as these from *Introduction to the Bodhisattva's Way of Life* (5:70):

> And I shall, in order to benefit all living beings,
> transform this body so that it grants every wish.

And (3:21):

> Like the earth and other great elements
> and like space itself,
> may I remain forever as sustenance
> to support the lives of boundless beings.[80]

All these meditations have their origins in the flawless words of the sūtras. The practice of giving away the body, for example, is described in the *Sūtra of Akṣayamati*:

> This body I shall give away to all beings, so that they may do with it as they will. The four great elements—the element of earth, element of water, element of fire, and element of wind—are employed by living beings, using various means, to various degrees, toward various ends, providing for various needs and various enjoyments. And in just the same way, I will provide this body of mine, which is composed of the four great elements, to sustain all beings, on a vast scale, by various means, to various degrees, toward various ends, providing for various needs and various enjoyments.

This describes the practice of offering the body as a whole, whereas the *Sūtra Requested by Nārāyaṇa* describes the giving away of its various parts:

> Beings, whosoever they may be, may take from me whatever they desire: Those who want arms may take my arms; those who want legs may take my legs; those who want eyes may take my eyes; those who want flesh may take my flesh; those who want blood may take my blood; those who want marrow may take the marrow from my bones; those who want limbs may take my limbs; and those who want a head may take my head.[81]

Then, regarding the giving away of one's possessions, the same sūtra says:

> Never mind these outer things, such as wealth, grain, gold, silver, jewels, ornaments, horses, elephants, chariots, carriages, towns, cities, hamlets, valleys, kingdoms, countries, palaces, markets,[82] slaves, workers, employees, sons, daughters, and servants. Whatever any being requires, for whatever purpose, I shall give them, each and every one.

Regarding the offering of sources of merit, the *Sūtra of the Vajra Banner of Victory* says:

> With these sources of merit, I bring to mind all those who might be benefited by such roots of virtue.[83]

And:

> May these sources of merit sustain and benefit all beings as pure and limitless Dharma. Then, may these sources of merit put a stop to beings entering the hells and cause them to avoid the great sufferings of the animal realm and the world of Yama.[84]

This describes how we give away our sources of merit in general, but the *Sūtra of Akṣayamati* describes in some detail how our sources of merit from the past, present, and future can be directed toward specific ends.

To meditate on these three types of giving separately like this is the tradition that has come down from the masters of the past. Nevertheless, for the benefit of those who prefer fewer sessions of visualization, I will now explain how to use a vast method of visualization in order to offer one's body, possessions, and sources of merit simultaneously.

In this, as in the practice described above, we begin by arousing the motivation of bodhicitta and so on, then bring to mind the logic behind the practice of giving, and consider that our body is blessed and transformed into nectar. Then we consider that our possessions and our sources of merit take on the form of light and gradually dissolve into the nectar. Through this, it is transformed into an inconceivably vast ocean of elixir, sumptuous in color, aroma, taste, and potency and a source of all that could be wished for. From this, like steam rising from the surface of a lake, there arises a great mass of light, which forms into clouds, filling the whole universe in every direction, throughout the whole infinity of space. From these clouds there falls an unimaginably vast shower of nectar, cleansing the whole outer and inner world of both saṃsāra and nirvāṇa, so that the environments, physical bodies, and enjoyments are transformed and become just like those of the Palace of Great Bliss within the heaven of Akaniṣṭha.

We consider that the rain of nectar falls within the sight of the *most honored guests of saṃsāra and nirvāṇa*, including, in particular, our root and lineage teachers, the assembly of yidam deities, buddhas and bodhisattvas, pratyekabuddhas and śrāvakas,[85] and members of the ārya saṅgha. It fills whatever vessels they are holding, and they partake of it gladly. Rapt with delight and immaculate bliss, all their enlightened aspirations are fulfilled entirely.

We then consider that the rain of nectar falls within the sight of the protectors, who are *guests invited on account of their qualities*, and who include within their ranks all the powerful, oathbound, blessing-granting guardians, both those within the world and those beyond it. By consuming the nectar, all their aspirations and wishes are fulfilled, their power and strength increase, and they apply themselves more diligently to the task of guarding the Buddha's teachings.

Then we consider that the rain of nectar falls within the range of the beings of the six classes, the *guests invited out of compassion*, from the peak of samsaric existence down to the lowest hells and including all those in the intermediate state. Through this, the suffering within their minds, as well as the destructive emotions that are its causes, the negative actions that are the contributing conditions, and the stains of the two kinds of obscuration, are all purified completely along with their seeds and underlying habitual patterns. Their minds are flooded with immaculate bliss, and they gain abundant qualities of learning and realization.

Then we consider that the rain of nectar falls just as before, in the vicinity of the harmful influences and obstructing forces, who are the *guests to whom we owe karmic debt*, the 80,000 types of obstructing forces, the 404 types of sickness, the 360 types of demon (*māra*), the fifteen great harmful influences[86] that strike children, those who inflict harm on all living beings, those who prey on beings' life force and vitality, those who crave flesh and blood, and all those with malicious intentions and vicious conduct. Through consuming the nectar, they are all satisfied, their wicked intentions and cruelty are pacified, all karmic debts are repaid, and any threats of vengeance are assuaged. Love, compassion, and bodhicitta are born within their minds. Physically and mentally, they experience immaculate bliss, and they begin to act for others' benefit.

Once again, clouds arise out of the ocean of nectar, emanating and gathering just as before, transforming into offerings for the *first* type of guest. For each and every recipient, the nectar rains down and transforms into an utterly pure buddha realm with a golden ground inlaid with lapis lazuli designs, soft and yielding underfoot. The whole realm is lit up by rays of light. There are mountains of precious stones and forests of trees that gleam with jewels. There are pleasure groves and ponds, elegant stairways, palatial houses, and thrones. There are silken drapes, canopies, pennants, parasols, streamers, garlands, fine clothes, fresh drinking water, bathing water, flowers, incense, lamps, perfumed ointments, food, music, all plentiful and of various kinds. In addition, there are the seven emblems of royalty, eight auspicious substances, and so on, all the offering substances of gods and human beings.

All these offerings are perfect in their appearance and in their sound, smell, taste, and texture. They all have the power to generate immaculate bliss. Increasing, they become inconceivably vast, like the magical manifestations that arise through the infinite samādhis of the bodhisattvas with mastery in meditation. In their compassion, all the guests partake of the offerings and, by doing so, are greatly pleased.

Then, once again, for the *second* type of guest, just as before, inconceivable clouds of outer, inner, and secret offerings arise, including all manner of abodes and palaces, thrones, clothing and ornaments, costly tributes and gifts of charity, sacred substances, and so on.

Then for the *third* type of guest, just as before, the offering is transformed into inexhaustible objects of enjoyment, including all that they wish for in terms of lodgings, friends, relations, rulers, guardians, allies, defenders, companions, servants, food, clothing, medicine, riches, grain, stores, treasures, and the like.

For the *fourth* type of guest too, just as before, the offering is transformed into an inconceivably vast supply of whatever is desired, such as flesh, blood, fat, bones, marrow, brains, bile, sense organs, vital organs, skin, hair, nails, and so on.

Once again, the clouds emanate and gather just as before, and an unimaginably vast rain of nectar showers down. From each droplet of nectar shines out inconceivable rays of light. On the tip of each light ray appear a multitude of lotus flowers, so numerous as to defy the imagination. In the heart of each lotus appear an inconceivable number of bodies just like your own. Each of these bodies appears before the *first* order of guests, presenting them with all kinds of offering substances and singing, in various melodies and tones, praises to their enlightened body, speech, mind, qualities, and activity. These emanated bodies also urge the honored guests to turn the wheel of Dharma, request them not to pass into nirvāṇa, and recount tales of their various enlightened deeds. As a result, the enlightened aspirations of the victorious ones are fulfilled. Among the noble beings on lesser stages, the followers of the Basic Vehicle all enter the Great Vehicle, and those on the lower bhūmis all attain the higher stages and complete the processes of abandonment and realization.

For the *second* type of guest as well, these emanated bodies make offerings and offer praise and encouragement, as a result of which the guests diligently apply themselves to their appointed tasks.

Then, we consider that our emanations offer Dharma teachings to the *third* type of guest, on a vast scale, according to their specific capacity, mentality, temperament, and habitual tendencies. To those best suited to the teachings leading to rebirth in the higher realms, they offer those teachings. Likewise for those who are suited to the teachings of the Śrāvaka Vehicle, Pratyekabuddha Vehicle, Bodhisattva Vehicle, profound teachings, and elaborate teachings, they cater for each and every one's individual needs. Through this, any lack of understanding, misunderstanding, or doubt in these beings' minds is dispelled, all those who lack faith are inspired with faith, all those who have not been brought to the teachings are brought to the teachings, all who have not been matured are matured, all who have not been liberated are liberated, and all who have been liberated only partially are now liberated to the fullest possible extent.

Then, for the *fourth* type of guest, consider that the emanations manifest in various guises, whether peaceful or wrathful, in whichever form is most effective for their subjugation. Those requiring wrathful subjugation are wrathfully subjugated, those requiring careful guidance are carefully guided, and all are set upon the path to liberation.

Throughout all these meditations, we must maintain the wisdom that is utterly free from the three conceptual spheres of subject, object, and activity.

As we visualize ourselves giving the gift of Dharma, we can recite verses from the scriptures.

At the end, we seal the practice purely with the dedication of merit and prayers of aspiration.

It is certain that practicing visualizations such as these, even for just a single session, will yield boundless merit. This is due to the extraordinary *field* of the practice, which includes all the most honored guests of saṃsāra and nirvāṇa, without exception; as well as the extraordinary *motivation*, which is comprised of love, compassion, and bodhicitta; the extraordinary *objects* of the practice, because we are giving away our body, possessions, and sources of merit in their entirety; the extraordinary *nature* of the practice itself, which makes use of skillful techniques of visualization on an incredibly vast scale; and the extraordinary *dedication*, which is pure, being entirely free from the three conceptual spheres.

Through these wonderful practices, we will swiftly accomplish the ability to benefit limitless beings directly, through the miraculous capacity that great bodhisattvas achieve through the power of their prayers of aspiration. We might wonder how this could be.

In the *Gaṇḍhavyūha Sūtra*, when the lay woman (*upāsikā*) Prabhūtā explains to Sudhana the qualities of the samādhi called the Inexhaustible Adornment to the Treasury of Merit in elaborate detail, she says, "Son of good family, stay for a while and you will see it directly." The moment she says this, through the force of her prayers of aspiration from the past, countless beings arrive from the east and other directions. The upāsikā Prabhūtā prepares all kinds of seats for them and offers them whatever food and delicacies they desire, all rich in taste and color and fragrance, so that they are satisfied completely. In the same way, she also satisfies and pleases them with drinks, delicacies, seats, couches, carriages, clothes, flowers, garlands, perfumes, incense, ointments, powders, jewels, ornaments, jeweled chariots, parasols, victory banners, pennants, and utensils. She satisfies the gods with the food of the gods, and for each of the various beings—nāgas, yakṣas,[87] gandharvas,[88] asuras, garuḍas, kiṃnaras, mahoragas,[89] humans, and nonhumans—she satisfies and pleases them with all manner of food fit for human and nonhuman beings. Yet after all this, the contents of the pots are not diminished, depleted, reduced, or exhausted; they never run out.

As we can see from such accounts, the method of practice given here is entirely in accord with the contents of this sūtra.

We might imagine that it is difficult to gain much merit born of generosity merely from our own imagination. But that is not the case. Why? Generally speaking, the most important agent of either virtue or nonvirtue is the mind, and in particular, as *Introduction to the Bodhisattva's Way of Life* (5:9–10) explains, there can be no doubt that the transcendent perfection of generosity depends on the mind:

> If the transcendent perfection of generosity
> means eliminating poverty from the world,
> then since beings are starving even now,
> how could former buddhas have perfected it?

> The transcendent perfection of generosity
> is a willingness to give away all things
> to all beings, together with its result.
> Hence it's nothing but a state of mind.

These visualizations therefore bring together flawless instructions from the vast words of the Buddha and advice contained in the various instructions of the mind-training tradition. Rather than imitating the frog who lived in a well and who tried to fathom the size of the ocean, we must put all our efforts into this practice with resolute faith and trust. Moreover, if we refer to *Samantabhadra's Prayer of Good Actions*, we will see that it describes precisely the kind of practice outlined here.

In order to remain mindful and aware of these practices, we can recite aloud and reflect upon the meaning of verses such as the following from *Introduction to the Bodhisattva's Way of Life* (3:11):

> My own body and all that I possess,
> my past, present, and future virtues—
> I dedicate them all, withholding nothing,
> to bring about the benefit of beings.

❦

Gaining control over the inexhaustible treasury of space,
satisfying all the honored guests of saṃsāra and nirvāṇa,
this practice for entering the ocean of activity on a vast scale,
a treasure producing all that could be wished for, I offer to the fortunate.

The practice of alternating

Primarily this refers to the practice of alternating the two sessions of visualization outlined above. In order to grow more familiar with this and make the practice more stable, we can consider that as we breathe in, we take on others' negativity and suffering in the form of black smoke,[90] and as we breathe out, we send out our own happiness and virtue so that it ripens on others. We can count the number of times we do this and repeat the process a hundred or a thousand times.

Some texts say:

Begin the process of taking with yourself.

This is a method whereby we gradually familiarize ourselves with the training by taking upon ourselves right now any karma that is certain to ripen later on in life and by taking on in this lifetime any karma that is destined to ripen in future lives.

In addition, this line can refer to the practice for overcoming our self-cherishing that is described in *Introduction to the Bodhisattva's Way of Life*, beginning with the following verse (8:140):

> Put yourself in the position of an inferior and so on,
> then regard your self as if it were someone "other,"
> and with a mind devoid of any other thought,
> cultivate feelings of envy, rivalry, and pride.

Conclusion

In short, unless we practice *taking*, we will not cut through the bonds of self-cherishing; unless we practice *giving*, we will not perfect the accumulation of merit; and unless we *alternate* these two, we will not easily become familiar with the practice. Therefore, we must make an effort to practice all three forms of meditation. This, as it has already been explained, is the sacred heart of the Mahāyāna path.

Moreover, the *Avataṃsaka Sūtra* says:

> I will consider that the pains of all living beings become my own, and I will transform myself so as to sustain them all.

The *Aspiration to Supreme Conduct* says:

> May the sufferings of beings in the hells and the world of Yama
> and the sufferings of those in the animal realm and of human beings,
> the great mass of all the suffering of living beings,
> fall entirely upon me, and may living beings be happy!

The *Aspiration of Maitrāyajña*[91] says:

> May the hosts of gods, demigods, and mahoragas
> throughout all the countless realms that exist,

from the summit of existence to the hell of Unrelenting Pain,
all find happiness, and may I take their suffering upon myself!

Introduction to the Bodhisattva's Way of Life (8:136) says:

In order to allay harms done to me, therefore,
and in order to pacify the sufferings of others,
I shall give myself up to others
and cherish them as I do my very self.

These quotations describe the method of meditation. As it also says
in the same text (8:156–57), we should understand the infallible results
of an altruistic mind:

Certainly, therefore, I must apply myself
fully to the task of benefiting others.
The Buddha's words do not deceive,
so I will see the benefits of this in time.

Had I practiced this way in the past
and undertaken actions such as these,
I could not possibly have ended up like this,
lacking, as I do, a buddha's perfect bliss.

We might think that it is impossible to reach such a state of mind and to
cherish others more than ourselves, but it is not. It can be accomplished
through the power of habituation. As *Introduction to the Bodhisattva's
Way of Life* (8:115) says:

Just as, through habituation, I have come to regard
this body, devoid of self, with the thought of "I,"
why should I not, through habit,
come to regard others equally as "I"?

❧ ❧

The attitude of cherishing oneself is the root of a hundred ills;
that which overcomes it through various techniques
and is the source of all happiness and virtue is altruistic bodhicitta;
strive therefore to cultivate it, all you diligent practitioners!

PRACTICE BETWEEN SESSIONS

The root text says:

The instruction for periods between meditation, in brief:
three objects, three poisons, and three roots of virtue.
In all activities, train by applying slogans.

Pleasant, unpleasant, and neutral objects—sights, sounds, and so on—cause us to feel attachment, aversion, or dull indifference. They can therefore be transformed into sources of virtue. Whenever we feel attachment, we can aspire to take upon ourselves the attachment of all beings and pray that they come to possess abundant sources of virtue, devoid of any attachment. The same principle applies to the other two.

In all our activities, we should train ourselves by applying slogans.[92] The *Precious Garland* (5:84) says:

May their misdeeds ripen on me
and all my virtues ripen on them.

And *Introduction to the Bodhisattva's Way of Life* (10:56) says:

May the pains of living beings
all ripen wholly on myself.

And may the bodhisattva saṅgha
bring about the happiness of all.

And Tutop Wangchuk:[93]

May the sufferings of all beings ripen on me,
and through my virtue, may they all find happiness!

These quotes apply to the training in the bodhicitta of exchanging ourselves and others. Moreover, the *Ornament of Mahāyāna Sūtras* (5:9) says:

Whenever the heirs of the victorious ones
encounter any objects in the sensory domain,
they respond appropriately for beings' benefit
according to the corresponding instructions.

This means we must practice according to the teachings of the *Sūtra of Completely Pure Conduct*. In order to explain this method concisely, we will follow the summary of this sūtra composed by the master Jñānagarbha:

When remaining at home, the bodhisattva should recite these words and contemplate them from the depths of his heart: "May all living beings take up residence in the city of great liberation!"

Likewise, when lying down to sleep, the bodhisattva should think, "May all living beings attain the dharmakāya of the buddhas!"

In the event of dreaming, the bodhisattva should think, "May all living beings recognize the dreamlike nature of all things!"

When waking, the bodhisattva should think, "May all living beings awaken from ignorance!"

When getting out of bed, the bodhisattva should think, "May all living beings attain the form kāya of the buddhas!"

When getting dressed, the bodhisattva should think, "May all living beings dress in the clothing of dignity and self-control!"

When tightening his belt, the bodhisattva should think, "May all living beings be connected with sources of virtue!"

When sitting down, the bodhisattva should think, "May all living beings find the vajra seat at the place of enlightenment (*bodhimaṇḍa*)!"

When leaning back, the bodhisattva should think, "May all living beings reach the bodhi tree!"

When lighting a fire, the bodhisattva should think, "May all living beings burn away the fuel of their destructive emotions!"

When the fire is burning, the bodhisattva should think, "May the fire of wisdom blaze in all living beings!"

When cooking, the bodhisattva should think, "May all living beings gain the nectar of wisdom!"

When eating food, the bodhisattva should think, "May all living beings gain the food of samādhi!"

When going outside, the bodhisattva should think, "May all living beings escape the city of saṃsāra!"

When going downstairs, the bodhisattva should think, "May I enter saṃsāra for the sake of all living beings!"

When opening the door, the bodhisattva should think, "May all living beings open the doorway to liberation!"

When closing the door, the bodhisattva should think, "May all living beings close the doorway to the three lower realms!"

When setting out on the road, the bodhisattva should think, "May all living beings set out on the path of the noble ones!"

When going uphill, the bodhisattva should think, "May I lead all living beings to the happiness of the higher realms!"

When going downhill, the bodhisattva should think, "May all living beings put an end to the lower realms!"

When meeting beings, the bodhisattva should think, "May all living beings meet perfect buddhahood!"

When putting down his feet, the bodhisattva should think, "May I entrust myself to the task of benefiting all beings!"

When lifting his feet, the bodhisattva should think, "May all living beings be brought out of saṃsāra!"

When seeing someone wearing ornaments, the bodhisattva should think, "May all living beings gain the adornments of the major and minor marks!"

When seeing someone without ornaments, the bodhisattva should think, "May all living beings come to possess the qualities of purification!"

When seeing any vessel that is full, the bodhisattva should think, "May all living beings be replete with enlightened qualities!"

When seeing an empty vessel, the bodhisattva should think, "May all living beings be devoid of faults!"

When seeing beings take delight, the bodhisattva should think, "May all living beings delight in the Dharma!"

When seeing beings who are displeased, the bodhisattva should think, "May all living beings take no pleasure in ordinary conditioned things!"

When seeing happy beings, the bodhisattva should think, "May all living beings gain all the necessities of happiness!"

When seeing beings who are suffering, the bodhisattva should think, "May the sufferings of all living beings be pacified!"

When seeing people who are sick, the bodhisattva should think, "May all living beings be freed from every sickness!"

When crossing over water, the bodhisattva should think, "May all living beings cross over the ocean of saṃsāra!"

When washing, the bodhisattva should think, "May all living beings be free from physical and mental impurity!"

When seeing a shrine or stūpa, the bodhisattva should think, "May I become an object of veneration for all living beings!"

When reciting the qualities of the buddhas, the bodhisattva should think, "May all living beings reach the transcendent perfection of inexhaustible qualities!"

This is how we should train our minds, selecting the words that are appropriate to any given task or situation. If we wish to see a more elaborate version we can look into the sūtra itself.

Maintaining the yoga of daily conduct like this will swiftly bring about boundless benefit for others. As the *King of Samādhi Sūtra* tells us:

This I will tell you, so please understand:
Whatever names people apply to things,
thoughts will conceive of them as such,
and mind will engage with them accordingly.

And the *Precious Garland*[94] also says:

Even if you lack the strength for altruistic action,
constantly develop this intention.
In those who have such thoughts,
bodhicitta will indeed be born.

᾿᾿᾿

Achieve the great purpose through this supreme alchemy,
this method for transforming into a treasury of virtue,
destructive emotions focused on deceptive objects,
and the whole mechanism of ordinary action.

8. Absolute Bodhicitta: Śamatha and Vipaśyanā

❦

An elaborate explanation of the underlying logic of this practice and the stages of the meditation can be found in texts such as my own *Perfectly Illuminating the Profound Meaning: Advice on the Great Middle Way beyond Extremes*.[95] Briefly however, Kamalaśīla's *Stages of Meditation II* says:

> Having generated relative bodhicitta in such a way, strive to arouse absolute bodhicitta.

We must exert ourselves, as this says, in practicing this profound path through study, contemplation, and meditation, because it is certain that this alone will counteract the darkness of the two kinds of obscuration, and unless we overcome these two kinds of obscuration we cannot possibly attain omniscience. As it says in *Introduction to the Bodhisattva's Way of Life* (9:54):

> Emptiness is the antidote to the darkness
> of both emotional and cognitive obscurations,
> So why would those who seek omniscience
> fail to meditate on it straightaway?

We might wonder what the nature of absolute bodhicitta is and how we cultivate it in meditation. *Stages of Meditation II* says:

Absolute bodhicitta transcends the mundane; it is beyond all conceptual elaboration; it is utterly clear; it is the absolute domain; it is stainless and unmoving, like a candle flame undisturbed by wind. Its achievement requires long training in the practices of śamatha and vipaśyana.

Maitreya's *Ornament of Mahāyāna Sūtras* (5:8) also says:

> Since there arises wisdom beyond any concept of things or
> events,
> it is asserted to be the absolute [bodhicitta].

As this says, its nature is the wisdom that directly realizes the natural simplicity beyond conceptual elaboration. It is realized through cultivating the samādhi that unites both calm abiding (*śamatha*) and penetrating insight (*vipaśyanā*). As *Introduction to the Bodhisattva's Way of Life* (8:4) says:

> Knowing that the destructive emotions are overcome
> through penetrating insight suffused with stable calm,
> first seek the peace of calm abiding,
> which is found in joy and nonattachment to the world.

The meditation on absolute bodhicitta is therefore divided into two parts: practice during the session and practice between sessions.

PRACTICE DURING THE SESSION

This has two parts: śamatha meditation and vipaśyanā meditation.

Śamatha meditation
This has three parts: (1) the prerequisites for śamatha practice, (2) how to place the mind on an object of focus, and (3) the measure of accomplishment.

THE PREREQUISITES FOR ŚAMATHA PRACTICE
Stages of Meditation II says:

> The prerequisites for śamatha meditation are: remaining in a conducive environment, having few desires and practicing contentment, not being involved in too many activities, maintaining pure moral discipline, and fully eliminating all conceptual thoughts involving attachment and so on.
>
> A *conducive environment* should be known by these five characteristics: (1) the ready availability of necessities like food and clothing, (2) the absence of hostile beings and enemies, (3) freedom from disease, (4) the presence of good companions who maintain moral discipline and hold similar views, and (5) few people present during the day and little noise at night.
>
> *Having few desires* means not being excessively attached to having only the finest quality things, such as monastic robes, or to having many of them. *Contentment* means always being satisfied with whatever monastic robes and so on one can find.
>
> *Not being involved in too many activities* means to avoid ordinary activities like trade and commerce, not to become too familiar with householders and monks, and to avoid entirely the practices of medicine and astrology.
>
> *Pure moral discipline* means that for both sets of vows,[96] the basis of training has not been violated through either natural or proscribed negative actions. Even if, through carelessness, some violation does occur, you must swiftly make amends by performing the proper practices with regret. Even though it is said of the śrāvaka vows that a defeat cannot be repaired, if you feel regret, are determined not to repeat the action in the future, recognize that whatever the state of mind the action was performed with, that mind lacks any real essence, and become familiar with the view that all phenomena lack

inherent identity, your moral discipline is said to remain entirely pure.

And:

For desires, by considering how they lead to many problems in this and future lives, related conceptual thoughts can be eliminated.

Having understood the nature of these prerequisites, we must set about acquiring them. For should we lack them, we will fail to accomplish the śamatha practice that delights the learned. As Atiśa Dipaṃkara said [in verse 39 of *Lamp for the Path to Enlightenment*]:

While lacking the elements of śamatha,
even by meditating with great effort
for many thousands of years,
we will not accomplish samādhi.

HOW TO PLACE THE MIND ON AN OBJECT OF FOCUS
Stages of Meditation II says:

When meditating, first complete any tasks that need to be done beforehand, such as going to the toilet. Then, in a pleasant location, free of disturbing noise,[97] think, "I shall lead all sentient beings to the essence of enlightenment," and with this, generate the great compassion of wishing to liberate all sentient beings. Then pay homage to all the buddhas and bodhisattvas of the ten directions by prostrating yourself so that five points of your body [the hands, knees, and forehead] touch the ground.

Before a painting or other image of the buddhas and bodhisattvas, make as many offerings and praises as you can. Confess your misdeeds and rejoice in others' merit.

Then sit on a comfortable seat, either in the full-lotus posture of Vairocana or the half-lotus posture. Your eyes should not be open too wide nor too tightly closed but focused on the tip of the nose. Do not bend your body forward or backward but keep it straight, and turn your attention inward. Rest your shoulders evenly, your head not tilted back or forward or to either side. Your nose should be in line with your navel. Rest your teeth and lips in their natural state, the tongue touching the upper palate. Your inhalation and exhalation should be just barely discernable, gentle, soft, and natural, without undue noise, effort, or agitation.

Then, as Lord Atiśa said [in *Lamp*, verse 40]:

> Upon an object of mind, whatever it might be,
> settle the mind in virtue.

This means that we practice by settling the mind on any object of focus, whether with or without attributes. This is explained in *Stages of Meditation II*:

> One way of doing this is to rest the mind on the form of the Buddha as one has seen it depicted or heard it described. As it says in the noble *King of Samādhi Sūtra*:
>
> > His pure body the color of gold,
> > beautiful is the Protector of the World.
> > Whoever visualizes him like this
> > practices the meditation of the bodhisattvas.
>
> In this way, settle the mind on your chosen object and then continually bring the mind back to this object in order to settle it again.

As this makes clear, we should focus the mind on the Buddha's form, and this will not only help us to accomplish śamatha but, as it says in the sūtras, will also bring the inconceivable benefits of recollecting the Buddha.

At that time, the methods of eliminating agitation and dullness are as described in *Stages of Meditation II*:

> Having placed the mind in this way, examine it and check whether it is properly focused on the object. Also check to see whether or not the mind has grown dull or has become distracted by wandering after external objects.
>
> If, as a result of lethargy or sleepiness, the mind is already dull, or if you suspect that dullness is approaching, turn your attention to a highly inspiring object, such as an image of the Buddha or a vision of light, and as dullness is dispelled, the object will be seen very clearly.

And:

> Whenever you notice that your mind has been sent racing by thinking about the qualities of outer objects, such as visual forms, or is thinking of something other than the object, or is agitated by desire for an object experienced in the past, or even if you suspect that distraction is approaching, turn your attention to objects that remind you of the impermanence and suffering and so on of all compounded things. This will calm the distraction and, with the rope of mindfulness and vigilance, bind the elephant of the mind to the tree of the object of meditation.
>
> Whenever you discover neither dullness nor agitation and the mind is naturally focused on its object, relax your effort and settle in equanimity, remaining for as long you desire.

The way to act during the period between sessions should be understood from the explanation given below.

THE MEASURE OF ACCOMPLISHMENT

The same text says:

> Know that śamatha is achieved when body and mind become
> extremely pliable and you have the power to direct your mind
> toward a given object just as you wish.

We might wonder why śamatha is called *calm abiding*. The same text
explains this very clearly, by saying:

> *Abiding* in a joyful and extremely pliable state of mind in
> which all distraction toward outer objects has been *calmed*
> and which remains focused inward, constantly and naturally,
> is called *calm abiding*.

We should understand, therefore, that states of mind that lack the faults
of meditation but in which this pliancy has not yet been attained merely
resemble genuine śamatha.

Vipaśyanā meditation

This has three parts: (1) the prerequisites of vipaśyanā, (2) how to practice it, and (3) the measure of accomplishment.

THE PREREQUISITES OF VIPAŚYANĀ

Stages of Meditation II says:

> What are the prerequisites of vipaśyanā? To follow a noble
> teacher, to seek extensive learning, and to contemplate in the
> proper way.

As this says, we must apply ourselves to following a qualified spiritual teacher, to acquiring extensive learning to the best of our ability,
and especially to studying and contemplating the scriptures and pith
instructions that teach the profound path. As Lord Atiśa said:

Life is short and there is much that could be known,
but since the exact length of our lives is uncertain,
earnestly, like swans extracting milk from water,
we must apply ourselves to our particular goal.[98]

HOW TO PRACTICE VIPAŚYANĀ

This has three parts: (1) eliminating conceptual constructs through the view, (2) taking to heart through meditation, and (3) enhancing through conduct.

Eliminating conceptual constructs through the view

This has three parts: (1) eliminating conceptual constructs regarding outer objects, (2) eliminating conceptual constructs regarding the mind, and (3) eliminating conceptual constructs regarding the antidote of meditation practice.

(1) Eliminating conceptual constructs regarding outer objects
The root text says:

Consider all things and events as dreamlike.

The meaning of this is explained in *Stages of Meditation II*:

> "Things and events" (or *dharmas*), in short, are comprised of the five aggregates, twelve sense sources (*āyatana*), and eighteen elements (*dhātu*). The physical aspects of the aggregates, sense sources, and elements are, in an ultimate sense, nothing other than aspects of the mind. When they are broken down into subtlemost particles, and these are examined to determine the nature of their parts, no real nature can be definitively identified.
>
> Therefore, through the force of age-old clinging to forms and so on, which are in fact unreal—just like the appearances in a dream—visual forms and the like appear to ordinary beings as if they were external to the mind. Yet we must

examine them, because on the ultimate level, these forms and such are nothing other than aspects of mind.

As this says, as a result of our habitual tendencies from waking life and through the contributing circumstance of being asleep, we may experience all manner of things in our dreams, yet nothing that we experience in the dream has even the slightest reality. In just the same way, through the habitual tendency—which has developed throughout beginningless time—of perceiving things as real, and through the contributing circumstance of our own karma, we experience a variety of objects. Although these appear to us to be more than just aspects of mind, it is certain that they do not have even the slightest reality.

(2) Eliminating conceptual constructs regarding the mind
The root text says:

Examine the nature of unborn awareness.

Stages of Meditation II says:

> When you consider how all the three realms are merely the mind, and you realize that this is so and that all imputed phenomena are really nothing other than the mind, then by examining the mind, you are examining the nature of all phenomena. Then analyze along the following lines. On the ultimate level, the mind too cannot truly exist. How can the mind that perceives the aspects of forms and so on—which are essentially unreal—and that appears in these various aspects ever be real? Just as physical forms and so on are false, since the mind is not separate from them, it too is false.
>
> When we examine the nature of mind with wisdom in this way, we find that ultimately mind is perceived neither inside nor outside. Nor is it perceived somewhere else. The mind of the past is not perceived; nor is that of the future. The mind that arises in the present too is not perceived. When the mind

is born, it comes from nowhere, and when it ceases, it goes nowhere. Mind is not apprehensible, it cannot be pointed out, and it is not physical.

As this says, when we understand that all appearances are the magical manifestation of mind, and we examine the essence of mind using ultimate analysis, we arrive at the certain conclusion that it is beyond all conceptual constructs, such as outer and inner; past, present, and future; arising and ceasing; and so on.

(3) Eliminating conceptual constructs regarding the antidote of meditation practice
The root text says:

Let even the antidote be freed in its own place.

Stages of Meditation II says:

> If, in this way, the fire of the awareness of things as they are can be ignited through precise investigation, then just like flames sparked by rubbing sticks together, it will consume the wood of conceptual thought. This the Buddha himself has said.
>
> In the noble *Cloud of Jewels Sūtra*, he said, "In order to be free of all conceptual constructs, the one who is skilled in discerning faults practices the yoga of meditation on emptiness. Such a person, through repeated meditation on emptiness, when searching thoroughly for the identity and nature of the objects of mind's distraction and delight, realizes them to be empty. When the mind itself is also examined, it is realized to be empty. When you search in every way for the nature of what is realized by the mind, this too is realized to be empty. Through realization such as this, you enter into the yoga of signlessness."

As this explains by drawing upon the sūtras, when we meditate, having analyzed both outer objects and the mind, if we become attached to the meditation that is the antidote, we must thoroughly investigate its essence, cause, and result and become certain that it is, and always has been, empty.

Taking to heart through meditation
The root text says:

Rest in the ālaya, the essence of the path.

Generally, there are many explanations of the *ālaya* (or "universal ground") as one of the eight collections of consciousness, but here, as in the teachings of the Lamdré tradition, it refers to *śūnyatā*, meaning the nature of awareness and emptiness, inseparably united. It is called the "universal ground" because it is the basis for all the phenomena of saṃsāra and nirvāṇa. Therefore, as Lord Atiśa said:

> In the nature of things, beyond all conceptual elaboration, consciousness too comes to rest, beyond all concepts.

In other words, when it is directed toward the "object," the nature of reality beyond the limitations of fixed ideas, the mind that is the "subject" enters a mode of utter simplicity, or freedom from concepts, by cutting through any fixed ideas in the way described above. When we enter this state of simplicity, we simply rest in meditative equipoise without any further analysis or evaluation, projection or absorption, effort and exertion, or the like.
Stages of Meditation II says:

> When entering in this way into the reality of the selflessness of individuals and phenomena, since there is no further analysis to be done, you gain freedom from concepts and evaluation. Mental activity enters, naturally and spontaneously, into a single experience that is beyond expression.

Without conceptualizing, remain in meditation with exceptional clarity regarding reality itself. And while abiding in that state, do not allow the flow of mind to be distracted.

The way to dispel dullness and agitation has already been described.

Enhancing through action
The root text says:

The seven and their processes are conceptual, so forsake them.

The seven, meaning the consciousness associated with the six senses, and the rigid idea of "I" and "mine," which is referred to as the emotional mind (Skt. *kliṣṭamanas*), together with their accompanying thought processes, are all said to be *false conceptual patterns*, as we find in Maitreya's *Distinguishing the Middle from Extremes* (1:8):

False conceptual patterns are the mind
and mental processes of the three realms.

Whenever our minds are like this, and we are caught up in thinking about various things or reacting to objects, we must avoid the tendency to perceive things as real or to cling to their reality. Instead, by thoroughly examining the essence of the objects that mind is directed toward and the thoughts themselves, we must decide that they are beyond any conceptual constructs. If we can familiarize ourselves with this and with the technique, by practicing it again and again, then all proliferation of conceptual thoughts will become a support for the arising of nonconceptual wisdom. That is why this is referred to as *enhancement*.

THE MEASURE OF ACCOMPLISHMENT
Stages of Meditation II says:

While focused in that state of śamatha, to analyze reality
is vipaśyanā.

And:

> Once we have achieved physical and mental pliancy, when
> abiding in that, having eliminated every other mode of
> thought, whatever is contemplated by the mind within the
> realm of samādhi is considered to be like a reflection. Within
> that domain of samādhi meditation, to regard these reflec-
> tions and discern the meaning of these objects of knowledge,
> to discern them thoroughly, understand them fully, analyze
> them fully, endure them, take delight in them, discern their
> distinctive features, observe them, and understand them is
> what is known as vipaśyanā. Thus the bodhisattva is skilled
> in the practice of vipaśyanā.

As this says by drawing upon the *Saṃdhinirmocana Sūtra*, vipaśyanā is
discerning wisdom that is built upon physical and mental pliancy. It is
called *vipaśyanā* (superior insight) because, with a capacity exceeding
that of other states of mind, it sees the nature of objects.

Śamatha and vipaśyanā, which have now been explained, must be
practiced as a unity. This is because each of them by itself will not fulfill the purpose of eliminating the destructive emotions, realizing the
nature of things, and so on. We must therefore acquire a detailed understanding, including the knowledge of how they are to be combined.
This has already been explained elsewhere.

PRACTICE BETWEEN SESSIONS

The root text says:

Between sessions, be a conjurer of illusions.

As this indicates, during all our activities between sessions, having first
aroused great compassion, we must work for the benefit of others, while
maintaining illusory mindfulness and vigilance. *Stages of Meditation
II* says:

Should you suffer from physical harm and the like, regard the whole world as similar to an illusion, a mirage, a dream, a reflection of the moon in water, or an optical illusion. And think: "Since they do not understand the profound teachings, these beings are overwhelmed by their emotions in saṃsāra." And by thinking, "However I can, I must help them to understand reality," arouse great compassion and bodhicitta.

And:

Then slowly rise from the cross-legged position and prostrate yourself before the buddhas and bodhisattvas of the ten directions. Make offerings to them and recite praises. Then make vast prayers of aspiration by reciting *Samantabhadra's Prayer of Good Actions* and so on.

This is the clear advice given by the great pandit Kamalaśīla through his great compassion in these and other such sacred glimpses of the path to liberation.

❧

Appearances, in all their variety, are mind's magical manifestation,
and the nature of mind is, and always has been, unborn.
To those with wisdom beyond duality and transcending concepts,
in whom this is realized genuinely and with certainty, I prostrate.

This concludes the main practice, which is cultivating the two aspects of bodhicitta. The remaining points were referred to by the followers of the great aural lineage as "subsequent points." It is said that their divisions and their sequence are not rigidly determined. In fact, there are even variations in the root verses, both in terms of number and sequence. What follows is according to the *Seven Points*.

9. Subsequent Points

———— ❧ ————

TRANSFORMING ADVERSITY INTO THE PATH OF AWAKENING

The root text says:

> **When all the world is overrun with evil,**
> **transform adversity into the path of enlightenment.**

When the wealth, resources, and power of the world are overrun with and oppressed by evil and destroyed, so that adverse circumstances descend like rain, instructions on transforming adversity into the path are of the utmost importance, because without them our practice might be lost to circumstances.

There are two parts to this section: transforming circumstances through our attitude and transforming circumstances through our actions.

Transforming circumstances through our attitude
TRANSFORMING ADVERSITY INTO THE PATH OF AWAKENING THROUGH RELATIVE BODHICITTA
The root text says:

> **Drive all blames into one.**
> **Meditate on the great kindness of all.**

As this says, whenever unwanted circumstances befall us, rather than laying the blame on others, we must remember that the source of all harm is our self-cherishing, as was explained earlier. *Introduction to the Bodhisattva's Way of Life* (8:154) says:

> This is the one who, hundreds of times
> in cyclic existence, has done me harm.
> Now, remembering these grievances,
> I will crush your selfish attitude.[99]

As this says, we must direct all blame exclusively toward our own self-cherishing. We must address it by saying, "Through your power, throughout the whole of beginningless time, I have been envious of those above and disrespectful to those below, and I have been competitive toward my equals. Through such intentions and through my actions, I have brought harm on others, as a result of which I will experience limitless sufferings in the three lower realms and elsewhere." *Introduction to the Bodhisattva's Way of Life* (6:42) says:

> In times gone by, I was the one
> who caused them similar harm.
> So now it is only right that I,
> an abuser of beings, should suffer.

So now that the time has come to distinguish friend from foe, and to recognize what is to be eliminated and what is the remedy for doing so, we must vanquish this source of all harm. *Introduction to the Bodhisattva's Way of Life* (8:169) says:

> The time when you could harm me
> has passed and now is here no more.
> I see you now! Where will you hide?
> I'll crush you in all your arrogance.

Recognizing self-grasping to be the real enemy, we must appreciate the kindness of all beings, beginning with those who do us harm, by considering the benevolence each of them showed us as our parents in the course of our past lives without beginning. Moreover, as we read in *Introduction to the Bodhisattva's Way of Life* (6:113):

> Given that a buddha's qualities are gained
> in dependence on ordinary beings and buddhas alike,
> what sense is there in honoring only buddhas
> while not respecting these ordinary beings?

As this says, for someone seeking buddhahood, buddhas and ordinary beings are of equal benefit, because just as qualities such as faith are gained in dependence on the buddhas, all the qualities and activities of the bodhisattvas such as love, compassion, bodhicitta, the six transcendent perfections, and the four means of gathering disciples are gained in dependence on ordinary beings. By reflecting on these reasons again and again, therefore, we must put our energy into the visualizations for giving and taking, knowing that whatever adversity befalls us, this will only enhance the precious bodhicitta of exchanging ourselves and others, like adding fuel to a blazing fire.

TRANSFORMING ADVERSITY INTO THE PATH OF AWAKENING THROUGH ABSOLUTE BODHICITTA

The root text says:

> **Meditating on delusory perceptions as the four kāyas
> is the unsurpassable protection of emptiness.**

When we are plagued by adversity, by remembering the problems caused by clinging to delusory perceptions as though they were real, and the benefits to be gained by realizing their lack of reality, we must recognize how all the phenomena of saṃsāra and nirvāṇa, including such adversity, are empty in terms of their essence, cause, and effect.

Through this approach, the adversity itself can contribute to enhancing our absolute bodhicitta.

The method here is what the masters of the past referred to as *recognizing the four kāyas* or *taking the four kāyas as the path*:

1. The absence of arising in the beginning is equivalent to the *dharmakāya*.
2. The absence of ceasing in the end is equivalent to the *sambhogakāya*.
3. The absence of remaining in the middle is equivalent to the *nirmāṇakāya*.
4. The indivisibility of these is equivalent to the *svabhāvikakāya*.

Recognizing and meditating on these four is understood to create the auspicious circumstances for accomplishing the four kāyas. These methods for recognizing and meditating upon the emptiness of adversity and so on are said to provide unsurpassable protection. As the *Verse Summary of the Perfection of Wisdom* says:

> Through four causes, the bodhisattvas who are skillful and strong
> prove difficult to defeat and immune to the four māras:[100]
> They abide in emptiness, never forsake ordinary beings,
> act according to their words, and possess the buddhas' blessings.

Transforming adverse circumstances through actions

The root text says:

The fourfold practice is the best of methods.

The four practices are as follows:

1. The practice of accumulating merit

Whenever suffering befalls us and we are bereft of happiness, by recognizing that this is because we lack a store of merit, which is the cause of happiness, we must put our energy into practices that will cause happiness, such as making offerings to the teacher and Three Jewels, venerating the saṅgha, offering tormas[101] to the elemental spirits, meditating on tonglen, and so on. Above all, we should make a maṇḍala offering to the teacher and Three Jewels and pray to them fervently, without any hope or fear, saying, "If it is better for me to be sick, bless me with sickness. If it is better for me to be healed, bless me with recovery. If it is better for me to die, bless me with death. If it is better for me to live, bless me with life..." and so on.

2. The practice of purifying misdeeds

Having understood, as explained in the teachings, the reasons we must abandon our misdeeds, which are the cause of our suffering, we must confess them to the fullest possible extent, using the four powers: to feel regret for the harmful actions we have committed in the past is the power of *remorse*; to vow never to repeat them even at the cost of one's life is the power of *turning from harm*; to take refuge and generate bodhicitta is the power of *support*; to meditate on emptiness, recite dhāraṇīs[102] and mantras, and so on is the power of *action as an antidote*. This is the most wonderful and supreme method of purifying negativity. As it says in the *Sūtra of Four Dharmas*:[103]

> Maitreya, if a person has these four dharmas, all the negative, harmful actions he or she has done will be cleansed and purified. What are these four? The power of support, power of remorse, power of turning from harm, and power of action as an antidote.

3. The practice of offering to harmful influences

Giving tormas to the harmful influences, such as the masters of sickness,[104] we entrust them with activity and meditate on tonglen, saying, "Thank you for spurring me on and supporting me in my training in the two kinds of bodhicitta. Still, I request you to cause the sufferings of all beings to ripen on me!"

4. The practice of offering to the Dharma protectors

Offering tormas to the Dharma protectors, we request them to pacify all circumstances that might hinder our cultivation of the two kinds of bodhicitta, to bring about favorable conditions, to transform adversity into the path, and to assist us so that throughout our lives we may arouse bodhicitta, maintain it, increase it further, and perfect it. Yet we must not request them to free us from illness or harmful influences or to bring us joy and happiness and so on, because by ourselves we do not know whether it is better for us to be sick or well, to live for a long or a short time, and so on. It is those who possess the eyes of wisdom, including the Dharma protectors, who know this directly.

Moreover, in order to integrate our immediate experiences into the path, we must do as the root text advises:

Whatever you encounter, apply the practice.

In all our actions, whether we are walking, moving around, lying down, or sitting, all that we encounter through our six senses will either be favorable or unfavorable. So we must never part from mindfulness and vigilance and offer all favorable circumstances to others, take all unfavorable circumstances on ourselves, meditate on emptiness, and so on.

Likewise the root text says:

When the two are complete, take on all.[105]

If we experience intense physical or mental suffering, such as leprosy or depression, and if we experience destructive emotions such as desire or anger that we cannot avert, by recognizing that countless other sentient beings have similar experiences, we take all of their negativity and suffering upon ourselves.

In short, the root text says:

Transform the unfavorable into supports for meditation.

We must put our energy into applying methods for transforming any unfavorable circumstances that might arise, such as outer injury or inner hurt, into supports for training in the two kinds of bodhicitta.

In particular, it is said:

First address whatever is most prominent.

When we understand that the most fundamental or prominent thing to eliminate is our own self-cherishing, in order to suppress or uproot it, we must practice in such a way that all Dharma, such as the two kinds of bodhicitta, functions as an antidote to self-cherishing.

If we take up the practice of these instructions on transforming circumstances, then, just as in the saying "When you have arrived at an island of gold and jewels, you won't find a stone to throw at a dog," it will be impossible for any thing or event to hinder our mind training. Therefore, in times of turbulent adversity such as these, we must practice it sincerely, applying all our energy.

APPLYING THE PRACTICE THROUGHOUT THE WHOLE OF LIFE

The root text says:

> **The essence of the instruction, briefly stated,**
> **is to apply yourself to the five strengths.**

1. The strength of impetus
This means to create a strong impetus in the mind by thinking again and again, "From now on, for this month, this year, throughout my life, and until I attain enlightenment, I will never part from the two kinds of bodhicitta!"

2. The strength of familiarization
This means training with great enthusiasm in the two kinds of bodhicitta, employing the full strength of your body, speech, and mind, with constant application, like the unending flow of a river.

3. The strength of wholesome seeds
This means creating as many sources of virtue as possible, by making offerings to the teacher and the Three Jewels and so on, all directed

toward the aim of arousing and further enhancing the two kinds of bodhicitta.

4. The strength of revulsion

This means to reflect again and again on the faults of a self-cherishing attitude, as they have already been explained, and on the serious harm inflicted by our self-clinging and other destructive emotions, which are our enemies, as *Introduction to the Bodhisattva's Way of Life* (4:30–31) says:

> Even if the gods and asuras
> were all to rise against me,
> they could not lead me down
> to the fiery hell of Unrelenting Pain.
>
> Yet these powerful foes, my own emotions,
> will cast me, in a single instant, to where
> even mighty Meru, the cosmic mountain,
> would be consumed and turned to ash.

The same text (4:32) also explains the long duration of such harm:

> No other enemy can harm me like this
> over such enormous lengths of time
> as do these foes, my destructive emotions,
> which have neither beginning nor end.

By calling to mind statements such as these, reflect again and again on the faults of self-clinging and so on.

5. The strength of aspiration

This means that following every act of virtue, we seal it by making a dedication of merit that is utterly pure, in the absence of the three conceptual spheres, and by making prayers of aspiration. In particular, we must put all our energy into making prayers such as, "In all my lives, may I never be separated from the motivation of twofold bodhicitta! Through my deeds of body, speech, and mind, my possessions and sources of merit, may I bring benefit to limitless beings! May I be able to transform all adversity into the path of awakening!" and so on. As it says in a sūtra:

> Everything is circumstantial
> and depends entirely on our aspiration.
> Whatever prayers of aspiration we make,
> the results we will gain accordingly.[106]

For the moment of death

We might wonder about the instructions for the moment of death according to this tradition. The root text says:

**The Mahāyāna advice for transference[107]
involves the same five strengths. Conduct is important.**

We must continually prepare ourselves for the moment of death, from now onward, by telling ourselves, "I will remember the instructions on the five strengths and the associated conduct at the moment of death!" and by putting this into practice whenever we fall asleep.

Practically, this means that when the moment of death arrives, we must apply ourselves to the intensive practice of these five strengths, especially the strength of wholesome seeds. For instance, we can practice the six transcendent perfections in the following way:

To make offerings to the Three Jewels without being attached to our possessions is the practice of *generosity*. To avoid being stained by impairments or downfalls, through repairing them, confessing, making pledges, and so on is the practice of *ethical discipline*. To forgive and heal any resentment that others may have toward us, and to feel no hostility toward anyone, is the practice of *patience*. To generate enthusiasm for virtuous practice, including mind training, is the practice of *diligence*. To rest in meditation on the two kinds of bodhicitta and so on is the practice of *meditative concentration*. To investigate the actual nature of things is *wisdom*.

The particular conduct to adopt is as follows. At the moment of death, we must lie on our right side, with our right hand supporting our right cheek. With the little finger of the same hand, we close the right nostril, so that we can breathe through our left.[108] We then pass away, focusing on whichever of the two kinds of bodhicitta we are most familiar with.

In short, the main obstacle at the moment of death is craving and attachment toward the homes, body, and possessions of this life, so we must make a great effort to renounce them. The way to do this, without concern for outer preparations or arrangements but through applying the instructions on mind training, is as follows: Recognizing the insubstantiality of all the objects of our desires and motivated by bodhicitta and so on, we can make the following aspiration, possibly even reciting it aloud: "All that I own—my home, my body, and my possessions—can be taken from me in any way, openly by force, sneakily by stealth, through deceit, or in any way at all, by enemies or relatives or those in between, yet whatever happens may these possessions of mine always be a cause of benefit and happiness!" This is the unsurpassable method for making our home, body, and possessions meaningful after we have passed away. So without neglecting what is of the utmost importance, we must be sure to remember it when the time comes.

❧ ❧

When the fierce winds of adversity rise up,
they transform them into supports for enlightened action,
applying the five strengths, the purest essence of the path—
these are the victorious buddhas' true heirs.

THE MEASURE OF MIND TRAINING

The root text says:

The measure of the training is in turning away.

As we turn away from ordinary attitudes and patterns of thought, we will naturally go through different experiences, according to the particular focus of each stage on the path. For example, the meditation on impermanence will turn our minds away from the pursuits of this life. Similarly, meditating on the effects of actions will turn our minds from nonvirtue. Meditating on the trials of saṃsāra will turn our minds from the whole of cyclic existence. Meditating on relative bodhicitta will turn our minds from the attitude of self-cherishing. Meditating on absolute bodhicitta will turn our minds from grasping at characteristics.

The root text also says:

A sign of proficiency is to have five greatnesses.

This means simultaneously being a great *bodhisattva*, who has the two kinds of bodhicitta, a great *upholder of the Vinaya*, shunning all forms of impairment and downfall, a great *ascetic*, practicing limitless austerities, a great *practitioner of virtue*, always diligent in applying oneself, and a great *yogi*, for whom both self and others, saṃsāra and nirvāṇa, are of a single taste.

In short, the root text says:

All teachings share a single objective.

All the teachings of the three vehicles share the common objective of overcoming ego-clinging. Therefore, by examining our own minds to see whether or not the practice is acting as a remedy for ego-clinging, we can determine whether or not we are proficient in bodhicitta.

We might wonder if other people's positive view of us is valid testimony, so the root text addresses this by saying:

Of the two witnesses, rely upon the principal one.

Even if fellow Dharma practitioners, as witnesses, are not offended by our actions, we should not consider their testimony to be the most important, because for the most part, they do not know our minds. Instead, without becoming too self-conscious, we should consider our own minds, once we have applied the Dharma, to be our principal witness. Our own minds, after all, are not hidden from us.

The root text also says:

Always maintain only a joyful attitude.

When we have the strength that comes from feeling assured that we will be able to transform any kind of adversity, then without any anxiety, we will be able to cultivate joy, no matter what setbacks might befall us.

The root text says:

If this can be done even when distracted, you are proficient.

Just as a skillful rider will not fall from his horse even if he is distracted by other things, whenever any adversity should arise, such as people suddenly harming us, if we are moved to feel compassion for our attackers, and our anger and so on cease even without us having to apply much effort, this is a measure of having trained the mind. Therefore when anything like this does happen, we must be joyful and inspired and continue exerting ourselves on the path.

THE COMMITMENTS OF MIND TRAINING

The root text says:

Train constantly in three basic principles.

These *three principles* are (1) not to transgress our mind-training commitments, (2) not to be reckless, and (3) not to fall into partiality.

1. Saying to ourselves, "We are practitioners of mind training so we must only guard the mind," we might ignore the other trainings, both major and minor. But we must let go of such notions and maintain all the trainings we have committed to undertake, without allowing any of them to decline.[109]

2. We must avoid all forms of reckless behavior intended to demonstrate to others that we have no self-cherishing, such as chopping down powerful trees or disturbing the waters of powerful lakes.[110] Instead we should follow the example of the masters of the Kadam tradition founded upon the teachings of the great Dromtön at Radreng Monastery.

3. We should avoid all forms of partiality, such as tolerating abuse from human beings but not from nonhuman beings, respecting the nobility but disrespecting the common people, and loving our friends but hating our enemies, and instead apply the training universally.

At that time, the root verses advise:

Change your attitude, but remain natural.

Mentally we must transform our attitude from one of self-cherishing to one of cherishing others, while in terms of our action, we continue to conduct ourselves in the same way as our Dharma companions. It is said that all mind-training practices should involve "making great progress but with few outward indications."

Moreover, the root text says:

Don't speak of injured limbs.

We should not speak about others' handicaps, such as their injured limbs.

In terms of our motivation, it says:

Don't ponder others' flaws.

We should not expend even a single moment contemplating the failings of other beings in general and those who have entered the Dharma in particular. A sūtra says:

> Consider all beings as your teacher.

We should train in pure perception and examine our own minds. The root text says:

> **Train first with the strongest destructive emotions.**

Setting aside all other practices, we must begin with the remedy that will help us to overcome desire or whichever is our strongest destructive emotion.

> **Abandon any expectations of results.**

We must let go of any expectations of gaining results for ourselves through the practice of mind training, such as gaining wealth and respect in this life, finding happiness in future lives as a god or human being, and ultimately gaining nirvāṇa.

> **Give up poisonous food.**

We must not contaminate our virtuous practices with the poisons of clinging to things as real or self-cherishing.
The root text says:

> **Don't be so loyal to the cause.**

We must not continue to hold grudges based on the harm others do to us.[III]

> **Don't lash out in retaliation.**

We must not retaliate against jibes made at our expense.

Don't lie in ambush.

We must not seek opportunities to take revenge.

Don't strike a vulnerable point.

We must not do anything to cause pain to others' minds by exposing their hidden faults, reciting the "life-force mantras" of nonhuman beings, and so on.

Don't transfer the ox's burden to the cow.

We must not pass on to others any blame or guilt that is ours alone.

Don't be competitive.

We must avoid any thoughts of trying to take for ourselves possessions or fame that are held in common and any actions based on such a motivation.

Don't misperform the rites.

Taking defeat upon ourselves with the wish that we will benefit in the long term or training the mind in order to pacify disease or harmful influences is like a mundane rite to avert misfortune and should be avoided.

Don't reduce gods to demons.

Relinquishing our pride and arrogance through mind training, whatever the company we keep, we should always regard ourselves as the lowliest of servants.

Don't seek others' misery as crutches of your own happiness.

We must avoid the attitude of wishing suffering upon others as a means toward securing our own happiness, as well as any actions based on such a motivation.

THE PRECEPTS FOR MIND TRAINING

The root text says:

Do everything with a single intention.

All daily activities of eating, dressing, and so on should be done purely with the intention of benefiting others.

Counter all adversity with a single remedy.

While we are practicing the path, whenever we encounter unwanted circumstances, such as ill health, harmful influences, hostile people, or an increase in the destructive emotions in our own mind, we can consider all the similarly unwanted and unfavorable circumstances that beings everywhere endure and take them all upon ourselves. In so doing, we resolutely turn our minds exclusively toward great compassion.

Two tasks: one at the beginning and one at the end.

At the *beginning* of the day, create a forceful intention in your mind, as already explained. At the *end* of the day, when you lie down to sleep, review the day and check whether you accomplished what you intended. If you did, you can rejoice; if you did not, confess your errors and so on. By doing this your mind will be following the course of the Dharma.

Whichever of the two occurs, be patient.

Whether we experience *prosperity* or *poverty*, we must transform everything into the path. By recognizing that the nature, causes, and conditions of such situations are all like illusions, we will avoid arrogance or despair.

Keep the two, even at your life's expense.

We must keep the commitments of the *Dharma in general* and *mind training in particular* even at the cost of our lives. Unless we do so, the roots of our practice will be spoiled, like a dilapidated old house with its foundations worn away.

Train in the three difficulties.

We must put our energy into the methods for remembering the antidotes to the destructive emotions, which is *difficult in the beginning*; averting the mental states that must be eliminated, which is *difficult in the middle*; and putting a stop to the flow of mental states to be eliminated, which is *difficult at the end*.

Acquire the three main provisions.

We must make an effort to secure the *outer provision*, which is following a spiritual guide, the *inner provision*, which is applying the Dharma to our minds, and the *outer and inner provisions*, which means gaining food and clothing and other factors that assist in the practice.

Cultivate the three that must not decline.

We must meditate continually on *devotion* toward the teacher, *enthusiasm* for the practices of mind training, and the *wish to keep the commitments* we have made, all of which should not decline.

Keep the three from which you must not separate.

We must ensure that our *body, speech, and mind* never deviate from virtue.

Apply the training impartially to all.
It is vital that it be deep and all-pervasive.

We must apply the mind training universally, without any partiality or discrimination between near and far, high and low, those who help and those who harm. Eventually the practice has to extend to all beings. This should not be mere lip service but genuine competence rooted deep within our being. This is vital for all the practices of the beginning, middle, and end.

Meditate constantly on those who've been set apart.

In our practice of mind training, we must focus especially on those we naturally dislike, such as difficult beings, rivals, those who harbor animosity toward us, those who repay our kindness with abuse, and those who bear grudges, as well as suffering beings, like the sick and unprotected, and those for whom our actions have more impact, such as our own parents. We must focus on them in our meditation and also help them directly in our actions.

Don't be dependent on external conditions.

Rather than being dependent on finding the right circumstances or avoiding unfavorable conditions, we must transform all that happens to us into the path.

This time, practice what's most important.

Now that we have this opportunity to practice the Dharma, there are six important things we must take to heart:

  1. It is more important to practice for the sake of future lives than for the present life.

2. It is more important to practice than to teach.
3. It is more important to train in bodhicitta than in other practices.
4. It is more important to focus on the teacher's pith instructions than on scripture and reasoning.
5. It is more important to stay in one place than to travel around.
6. It is more important to apply the antidotes than to avoid whatever provokes disturbing emotions.

The root text says:

Don't misunderstand.

We must avoid six kinds of misunderstanding:
1. Misplaced *patience* is to bear the suffering involved in protecting our friends and outdoing our enemies but not the difficulties involved in practicing the Dharma.
2. Misplaced *intention* is to have no interest in the Dharma of transmission and realization but to take an interest in the glories and riches of this life.
3. Misplaced *relish* means that rather than savoring the practice, we savor worldly pleasures.
4. Misplaced *compassion* is to cultivate compassion for those who endure hardship for the sake of the Dharma but not for those who inflict great harm on others.
5. Misplaced *pursuit* is to try to achieve greatness in this life rather than striving in practice.
6. Misplaced *joy* is to feel joyful at the sufferings of those who harm us rather than cultivating joy for others' happiness and virtue.

Avoiding these six, we must take to heart their opposites, the six correct forms of practice.

The root text also says:

Don't be inconsistent.

Rather than practicing sporadically, as if only to fulfill an obligation or only in strict sessions, we must train uninterruptedly, everywhere and on every occasion.

Train wholeheartedly.

Instead of entertaining lots of plans and speculations, we must devote our attention to the practice of mind training.

Gain freedom through discernment and analysis.

We will be freed from the tyranny of destructive emotions by analyzing our minds again and again to determine whether the study, reflection, and meditation we have done has served to remedy our destructive emotions, whether we are sincere in our speech and thoughts, and so on.

Don't be boastful.

We must not boast to others in any way about how we have helped others or about the practice we have done and so on.

Don't be irritable.

Whenever we are harmed by others, through their spiteful words or behavior or in any other way, we must not be short-tempered or strike back.

Don't be temperamental.

When we are in others' company, we should avoid suddenly switching from a mood of cheerfulness to one of displeasure.

Don't seek acknowledgment.

In all our practice, which is focused primarily on benefiting others, we must be free from any expectation of the slightest renown, approval, or expression of thanks, even somebody saying, "Well done!"

In conclusion, we must follow these guidelines and trainings correctly, and we must take every opportunity, both during the meditation sessions and outside them, to apply the methods that will cause the two kinds of bodhicitta to develop and expand like a river in summertime.

⁓✻⁓

Forever turning your back on thoughts and deeds rooted in delusion, to set out, naturally and spontaneously, on the path of the Great Vehicle and to maintain its general and particular precepts and commitments so they remain undiminished—this is the way to delight the victorious ones.

10. Conclusion

The root text says:

> This essence of the nectar-like instructions
> for transforming into the path of awakening
> the five prevalent signs of degeneration
> was passed down from the one from Golden Isle.

In this age, the text says, when the five signs of degeneration—in time, beings, lifespan, destructive emotions, and view—are extremely widespread, there are few circumstances conducive to happiness and many that provoke suffering; thus we must apply the key points of this extraordinary instruction on transforming circumstances. This quintessential nectar-like instruction for transforming all adversity into the path of awakening, like turning poison into medicine, was transmitted mainly through the lineage of the great learned master of Suvarṇadvīpa.

This concludes the vajra verses of the aural lineage that originated in India. The text continues:

> When karmic seeds left over from former trainings
> were aroused in me, I felt great interest, and so,
> without regard for suffering or disparagement,
> I sought instructions on subduing ego-clinging.
> Now, even in death, I will have no regrets.

In other words, the great Chekawa endured many hardships in order to receive these instructions and put them into practice. Through them he came to master the bodhicitta of cherishing others more than himself, giving him great joy and confidence. The root verses given earlier all come from the aural lineage, but it was mainly Chekawa who set them down in writing.

Anyone who practices this mind training, by following its preparation, main part, and conclusion, will be able to transform even the conditions for suffering into causes of happiness, so that even one's body could be called "a great city for producing happiness."

This instruction for meditating on bodhicitta
brings all other works together in one.
By following it, with effort and in all situations,
we'll perfectly fulfill our own and others' aims.

The great ocean of the Omniscient One's excellent teachings, vast and
    deep,
was churned by the wind of the diligent application of critical analysis
to produce this sublime stream of nectar, these immaculate
    instructions,
which now flow clearly into valleys beneath the snow-capped
    mountains.

This is the ultimate enlightened wisdom of all the buddhas.
This is the ultimate point of entry for all the buddhas' heirs.
This is the ultimate quintessence of all collections of the teachings.
This is the ultimate source of vitality for all who live.

This is a joyous celebration created especially for the fortunate,
who seek to heal the sickness of destructive emotions in every living
    being,
eliminate the stains of every fault,
and enjoy the splendor of immortality and bliss.

The weak-minded are trapped within the cavern of wrong views,
never seeing the thousandfold light of these excellent teachings
nor tasting the river of immaculate nectar.
Alas! How are they ever to find benefit?

The sun of Buddha's teachings is obscured by the western mountains
    of time,
the eyes of beings' intelligence are clouded with partiality,
and the virtue and goodness of the world is destroyed by evil forces
    leading us astray—
in times like these, what use is all my striving?

Yet in response to the persistent requests
of a great many devoted students,
I, Künga Yeshé Palzangpo, upholder of the teachings,
composed this with a mind of love.

If it is found to contain any errors or omissions
or to be untimely—whatever mistakes I may have made
I confess before the hosts of buddhas and their wise heirs:
May I be forgiven, and, through their kindness, purified.

Any virtue gained through these excellent explanations offered with
    the purest motivation,
I dedicate toward all living beings, as numerous as space is vast.
May they never be separated from bodhicitta
and swiftly reach the level of the Sovereign of Dharma.

This instruction on Mahāyāna mind training entitled "The Stream
of Nectar" was composed in the mountain hermitage of Great Bliss
(Dechen) by Künga Yeshé, the monk who teaches the Dharma, who
has bowed his head reverently before the feet of many great masters
embodying limitless wisdom and love, and who has long savored the
nectar of their teachings. The scribe was the monk Tsültrim Gyaltsen,

who is extremely devoted to this path and rich with the splendor of many qualities, such as faith, diligence, and intelligence.

May this be a cause for the precious teachings of the buddhas to spread in all directions and to remain long into the future!

Śubham. Virtue! Virtue! Virtue!

Appendix

❦

THE EXCELLENT PATH TO ENLIGHTENMENT
AN ASPIRATION PRAYER FOR MAHĀYĀNA MIND TRAINING

Homage to the guru!

Always loving toward beings and never untimely,
victorious buddhas and your heirs—think of me, I pray!
Grant your blessings, so that these, my heartfelt aspirations
to train and follow in your footsteps, may come true!

With compassion for all beings, limitless in number,
and devotion born of faith and understanding,
may I take refuge, from now until enlightenment,
with trust in the teacher and the Three Jewels!

This human form, so difficult to find, will not last long;
no matter where I'm reborn, there'll be no chance of happiness;
and positive and negative actions bear their fruits unfailingly—
seeing this, may I devote myself wholeheartedly to the sacred Dharma!

As it is a medicine to soothe all the pains of saṃsāric existence,
a supreme treasure bringing benefit and happiness to all,
and a gentle mother nurturing the buddhas and their heirs,
may my confidence in bodhicitta remain forever steadfast!

Never proud, no matter how prosperous I become,
and never despondent, even in dire misfortune,
this vast strength of mind possessed by bodhisattvas—
may it take birth definitively in my heart!

As it is the very essence of all the teachings,
the single path followed by all of Buddha's heirs,
and the guide and teacher to all who are enlightened,
may bodhicitta arise swiftly in my own mind!

These dream-like phenomena, delusory perceptions of my mind,
are unborn and beyond all conceptual elaboration.
Seeing this, during the post-meditation, through illusion-like
    concentration,
may I benefit these beings, figments of my own delusion, on a vast
    scale!

When seeing my companions, so kind and helpful to me in the past,
sinking now in this vast ocean of suffering,
may my mind be filled with love and tenderness for all,
like a mother watching helplessly as her beloved child is swept away
    and drowned!

May I take upon myself the harms and sufferings of beings,
my own mothers and fathers from lives without beginning,
and may I give away my own happiness and virtue to others,
so that this noble attitude, taught to be supreme, is ignited in my
    mind!

May whatever appears, the basis of destructive emotions like
    ignorance, desire, and anger,
whether it be friendly, hostile, or neutral,
become a support for bodhicitta,
like fuel heaped upon a blazing fire!

As it is the cause of all the destructive emotions that bind us in
    saṃsāra,
the source of negative karma and the various forms of suffering,
and a demon that obstructs us on the path to enlightenment,
may I firmly uproot all forms of self-cherishing!

Like perceiving nectar as pus as a result of karma,
the faults I see in others reflect my own impure perception.
Knowing this, may I be respectful to all other beings,
sources of ocean-like qualities of happiness and positivity!

Suffering, disdain, slander, and the like,
whatever unwanted circumstances befall me,
by seeing them as a support for the bodhisattva training,
may I accept them all with a mind of perfect joy!

The bounties of this world are like the stuff of dreams—
however many I acquire, may I never be attached to them,
and while seeing them as a means of benefitting others,
may I not be afraid to sacrifice even life and limb!

Should even my oldest and dearest of friends
turn against me and regard me as an enemy,
may I respond only with love and strive to bring about
their benefit and happiness, now and in the future!

Should hordes of demons craving flesh and blood
descend upon me, intent on devouring this illusory body,
still may I not succumb to thoughts of self-cherishing
but, with love, strive to bring them only benefit!

Seeing that these various phenomena do not ever part
from mind's nature, which is, and always has been, peaceful,
may deluded perceptions of adversity, like the moon's reflection,
lead me to a clear realization of the actual nature of reality!

Seeing all harm-doers as spiritual friends,
all suffering as adornments for the mind,
and all adversity as incitement to virtue,
may unfavorable circumstances be transformed into the path!

Knowing that hankering after my own happiness is the true enemy,
may ordinary adversaries become supports for awakening!
And, seeing sickness as a means of purifying negativity,
may unfavorable circumstances be transformed into the path!

Seeing evil omens as circumstances for attracting prosperity,
evil spirits as supports for gaining accomplishment,
and evil companions as a way of deepening my understanding of
    mistaken practice,
may adverse circumstances be transformed into the path!

Knowing what to take up and avoid, I shall accumulate and purify
    correctly,
pleasing the guardians will bring victory over obstacles and māras,
and through skillful means, all types of hindrance will become
    supports—
may I take to heart the four kinds of practice!

With sheer delight, may I don the armor of commitment[112]
and train the mind in the Dharma that subdues self-clinging!
With the support of wholesome methods and aspirations,
may my practice of Dharma equal the length of my life!

With the devotion of constantly recalling the guru
and perfect familiarity with bodhicitta, absolute and relative,
while never straying from the Dharma that is profound and vast,
may I have the merit to face death in this way!

Even though I be assailed by humans and nonhuman demons,
tormented by a disturbance in the body's elements,

or afflicted by intense destructive emotions,
may supreme bodhicitta never be diminished!

Even as the bardos' horrors unfold within my deluded perception,
or as I enter a future mother's womb, or later, during other lifetimes,
may I never forget, even for so much as a single instant,
the essence of Dharma—bodhicitta, precious and sublime!

The victorious buddhas and their heirs, the spiritual friends,
proclaim this excellent, genuine path to their circles of disciples.
Serving such teachers throughout all my lives to come
and embracing this instruction, may I benefit others!

By subduing self-clinging, may whatever I do become the Dharma!
Banishing hope and fear, may whatever happens be supportive!
By mastering the altruistic attitude, even if I should suffer,
may it only contribute to others' happiness and joy!

Never contaminated by the poison of clinging to beliefs
nor bound by compassion that is limited and partial,
may precious bodhicitta, uniting relative and absolute,
dispel all the ills of both existence and quiescence!

Even if my actions of body and speech are ordinary,
may I never be separated from the mind of bodhicitta!
Even without a routine of contrived virtuous actions,
through motivation's power, may I gather merit in abundance!

Though I dedicate my body, life, possessions, and merits of
    past, present, and future
each and every day for the good of all who live,
may hopes of gaining some benefit or happiness for myself in
    return
never occur to me, even for an instant!

To take defeat upon myself and give the victory to others,
to keep the lowest place and respect each and every being,
to offer only benefit in response to any harm that's done:
This is the discipline of the bodhisattvas—may I embrace it!

Respecting the teachers and taking to heart all that they say,
bringing together all the teachings in a single practice,
and abandoning hope and fear, may I always, for the sake of others,
clothe myself in the armor of enthusiastic diligence!

If it should prove to be a cause of harm to others,
may I abandon like chaff[113] even the bliss of liberation!
If it should benefit others, may I be born in the lower realms,
entering happily, as if strolling into a pleasant garden!

Guarding the three trainings as though they were my very eyes,
may my body, speech, and mind never waver from the Dharma,
and may I dedicate all my merits of the past, present, and future
purely, free from the three concepts of subject, object, and action!

With a mind filled with joy, may I enter
the ocean of conduct, vast and limitless in depth,
the mine of many million jewels of virtue and goodness
and the source of powerful accumulation![114]

When oppressed by the burden of all manner of sufferings,
through this particular remedy, out of all the countless skillful
    methods,
may I bring benefit and happiness to all beings without exception
and gain great powers of samādhi meditation!

Enlightened vision and actions are like a vast ocean, impossible
    to fathom;
so, having gathered within the great lake-like vessel of my own mind

rivers of treasure-like qualities drawn from an infinite sea of victorious
   buddhas,
may my own actions be indistinguishable from the ocean of enlightened activity!

*This prayer, incorporating the uncommon terminology of the Mahāyāna
mind-training teachings in verses of aspiration, was composed by the one
who has a heartfelt trust in this teaching, Lodrö Shenpen Dawa.*[115] *May it
be virtuous and auspicious!*

Notes

❧ ⁹℣ ❧

1 The precise number and sequence varies in different texts. Ga Rabjampa's root text, for instance, contains lines found in neither the *Root Lines of Mahāyāna Mind Training* nor the *Seven-Point Mind Training* texts in Jinpa 2006.

2 Sechilpuwa is also known as Chökyi Gyaltsen. Thupten Jinpa (2006: 11–12) lists the twelve most popular commentaries in Tibet as:

1. Sechilpuwa Özer Zhönu's commentary compiled from Geshé Chekawa's own lectures
2. Gyalsé Tokmé Zangpo's (fourteenth century) commentary
3. Zhönu Gyalchok's (fourteenth century) *Compendium of All Well-Uttered Insights*
4. Müchen Könchok Gyaltsen's (fifteenth century) *Supplement to the Oral Tradition*
5. Radrengpa's (fifteenth century) *Stream of the Awakening Mind*
6. Hortön Namkha Pal's (fifteenth century) *Mind Training: Rays of the Sun*
7. The First Dalai Lama Gendün Drup's (fifteenth century) *Lucid and Succint Guide to Mind Training*
8. Khedrup Sangyé Yeshé's (sixteenth century) *How to Integrate into One's Mind the Well-Known Seven-Point Mind Training*
9. Kalden Gyatso's (seventeenth century) *Dispelling the Darkness of Mind*
10. Yongzin Yeshé Gyaltsen's (eighteenth century) *Essence of Ambrosia*
11. Ngülchu Dharmabhadra's (eighteenth century) *Heart Jewel of the Bodhisattvas*
12. Jamyang Khyentsé Wangpo's (nineteenth century) *Seeds of Benefit and Well-Being*

3 This biography is based on the recently published "Shower of Blessing Elixir" (*Byin rlabs bdud rtsi'i char 'bebs*) composed by Khenpo Jamyang Sherap in 1998. See *Bdag nyid chen po gzhung lugs rab 'byams pa kun dga' ye shes kyi rnam*

par thar pa ngo mtshar sprin dkar gzhon nu'i rol rtsed byin rlabs bdud rtsi'i char 'bebs in Ga Rabjampa 2005: 308–80.

4 See, for example, Van Schaik 2011: 85–113, where the "golden age" covers the period 1315–1543.

5 *Sga stod mdzo nyag.*

6 A ḍākinī (Tib. *Mkha' 'gro ma*) can be either a female practitioner who has reached the highest level of attainment or a female deity in a pure celestial realm.

7 *Smra sgo mtshon cha.*

8 Elemental spirits (Tib. *'byung po*), associated with the elements of earth, water, fire, wind, and space, are said to cause harm and disease. They belong to the *preta* realm.

9 Another name for Vajrayāna or tantric Buddhism.

10 This is the master who, together with his student Könchok Gyaltsen, compiled the *Mind Training Collection* (*Blo sbyong brgya rtsa*) translated by Thupten Jinpa (2006).

11 The six basic treatises of the Kadampas are: (1) the *Udānavarga* and (2) *Jātaka* to inspire faith; Śāntideva's (3) *Śikṣāsamuccaya* and (4) *Bodhicaryāvatāra* to teach conduct; and (5) Asaṅga's *Bodhisattvabhūmi* and (6) Maitreya's *Ornament of Mahāyāna Sūtras* to teach meditation.

12 Ga Rabjampa was among the first to receive this title. According to Dreyfus (2003: 144), the title of Rabjampa was first awarded to Sangyé Pal, another disciple of Ngorchen Künga Zangpo. As Dreyfus notes, Rabjampa literally means "one who has studied extensively" and it "indicated the mastery of a large number of texts."

13 These teachings possibly served as the basis for the present volume.

14 Jyekündo Döndrup Ling. See description of Dezhung Rinpoche's visit there in Jackson (2003), p. 30. Jackson says it was the largest monastery in Gapa and housed about eight hundred monks.

15 The word *gandhola* is derived from *gandha* "incense." Like the Mahābodhi Temple in Bodhgaya, it is a shrine building primarily for offerings rather than assemblies.

16 It is said that Nāgārjuna also brought back special clay from the realm of the *nāgas*, or serpentine spirits, when he retrieved the Perfection of Wisdom sūtras. The clay was then used in the construction of temples and stūpas.

17 "Uncle and nephew" (*khu dbon*) refers to Ga Anyen Dampa Künga Drakpa (1230–1303), a disciple of Sakya Paṇḍita, and his nephew or descendant, referred to in the text as Drungchen Rinpoche.

18 Ga Rabjampa's nephew and disciple.

19 Sogyal Rinpoche 2002: 155.

20 Most versions of the *Seven Points* have *gang ba'i* meaning "full," but this text has *khol ba'i*, which according to Khenpo Appey Rinpoche (hereafter KAR) literally means "oppressed by."

21 Thupten Jinpa and others take *spyod lam* to refer to the practice of the five strengths, but the commentary here relates it to conduct, and specifically the posture one adopts at the moment of death.

22 The Tibetan text says *chos kun dgongs pa gcig tu 'dus*. Other versions have *dgos pa* (purpose) in place of *dgongs pa*, translated here as objective.

23 Literally, "Don't transfer the *dzo*'s burden to the ox." A *dzo* (*mdzo*) is a cross between a yak and a cow. Here we have followed Trungpa's "meaning translation."

24 This translation follows Khenpo Appey Rinpoche's explanation as *zur du bkol ba* and the commentary of Ga Rabjampa that follows.

25 On the meaning of this term in Tibet, see Jinpa 2006: 594–95n240.

26 On these three transmissions, see Jinpa 2006: 8–9.

27 Skt. *Sahāloka*. The name given to our world system, in which the Buddha manifested. It is said to be so called because beings here "patiently endure" the destructive emotions.

28 Literally, 9.9 million treatises (*gzhung lugs 'bum sde dgu bcu go dgu zhal ton du mdzad pa*).

29 The southern continent of Jambudvīpa is one of the four main continents according to the ancient Indian view of the world. In some contexts it would seem to refer exclusively to the Indian subcontinent, while at other times it refers to our world as a whole.

30 The first bodhisattva level or *bhūmi*.

31 Vimuktisena's famous commentary on the *Abhisamayālaṃkāra* relates it to the *Perfection of Wisdom in 25,000 Lines*.

32 That is, the *Perfection of Wisdom in 8,000 Lines*.

33 Believed by most scholars to be identified with Sumatra, but possibly Java or Malaysia.

34 A *yidam* (Skt. **iṣṭadevatā*) is a meditational deity and an essential support for Vajrayāna practice. Having made a connection with a particular yidam, as a result of past karma, the practitioner visualizes the deity and recites the appropriate mantra during meditation practice, before eventually recognizing the deity's enlightened qualities within him- or herself, and ultimately recognizing the inseparability of the deity from the nature of his or her own mind.

35 *Tīrthika* refers to proponents of non-Buddhist tenets, who are said to fall into either of the two extremes of nihilism or eternalism.

36 Literally: "their pillows joined together."

37 A form of Avalokiteśvara.

38 That is, Dromtönpa Gyalwé Jungné.

39 A.k.a. Künga Gyatso.

40 Kazhipa (*bka' bzhi pa*) is a title indicating that he had mastered four important texts. (KAR)

41 Ga Rabjampa refers to him by the Sanskrit equivalent of his name, Jñānaśrī.

42 *Saṃsāra* is the cycle of conditioned existence, birth and death, characterized by suffering, in which we are continually reborn until attaining nirvāṇa.

43 The seven points represent Mount Meru, the four continents, the sun, and the moon.

44 The *preta*, or "hungry ghost," is one of the six classes of existence within saṃsāra and is characterized by continuous hunger and thirst.

45 Great Fruition (Bṛhatphala) is one of the heavens of the third dhyāna level of the form realm.

46 An *uḍumbara* flower is a common symbol of rarity in Buddhist texts, as—at least according to some sources—it is said to appear only once every three thousand years.

47 *Asuras*, or demigods, comprise one of the six classes of existence described in more detail later in the text. A *garuḍa* is a mythical bird-like creature. A *vidyādhara* is a realized being who has mastered the power of awareness. A *kiṃnara* is a creature somewhat similar to a human being in appearance. *Uragas* are serpent-like spirits.

48 *Nam mkha' la ni 'chel.* The translation is tentative here, and based on commentary by Alak Zenkar Rinpoche (AZR).

49 This verse has been attributed to many authors. Jinpa (2006: 643n905) notes that it appears in Vasubandhu's commentary to his own *Treasury of Abhidharma*.

50 See Patrul Rinpoche 1994: 124. The nāga king Elapatra is reborn as a huge serpent whose head is crushed by an *elapatra* tree as a result of breaking his vows in a previous life when he angrily cut down a tree on which his robe had caught.

51 Patrul Rinpoche 1994: 123. King Māndhātṛi was reborn as a powerful universal ruler as a result of offering four beans to the Buddha Kṣāntiśaraṇa.

52 *Mjug.* La Vallée Poussin (trans. Pruden) has "consecutive." See p. 700.

53 The translators of Jamgön Kongtrul (2007: 319n228) note that this does not appear in the *Ratnāvalī* and they were unable to locate it elsewhere. It is curious that both Ga Rabjampa and Jamgön Kongtrul attribute it to that source.

54 The powers of support, regret, resolve, and action as an antidote.

55 Padmakara's version (2005) begins with *des pa*, but this says *nges pa*.

56 Ārya (Tib. *'phags pa*) or sublime beings have attained a degree of realization through reaching the path of seeing that is said to make them more "exalted" (the literal meaning of *'phags pa*) or "noble" than ordinary beings.

57 Avīci is the lowest and most fearful of the hot hells, as indicated by its name, which translates as Unrelenting Pain. See below for details.

58 Literally "a place of birth such as the womb" referring to the other modes of birth: from an egg, from heat and moisture, or miraculously. It is clear from the context however that this is primarily referring to birth from a womb.

59 Tib. *spra ba*; that is, *Artemisia vulgaris*, the plant used in moxibustion. (AZR)

60 The four seals (Tib. *sdom bzhi*) are axiomatic hallmarks of the Buddha's teachings. They are: "All that is conditioned is impermanent. All that is tainted is suffering. All phenomena are empty and devoid of self. Nirvāṇa is peace." It is often said that the real mark of a genuine follower of the Buddhist teachings is that he or she accepts these four.

61 The Yama world is an alternative name for the pretas' realm.

62 The meaning of *rnyod* here is unclear.

63 *'Dzol*. The meaning of this term is uncertain. It is possibly a scribal error. (AZR)

64 A unit of measurement somewhat similar to a league. In the Abhidharma literature one *yojana* is the equivalent of approximately four and a half miles.

65 An ancient measure named after the ancient Indian kingdom of Magadha.

66 *Saṅgharakṣitāvadāna*. This story of Saṅgharakṣita and further details of the sufferings of these hells are to be found in *Divine Stories: Divyāvadāna*, vol. 2 (Boston: Wisdom, forthcoming).

67 Ethical discipline, meditation, and wisdom.

68 Generosity, ethical discipline, patience, diligence, meditation, and wisdom.

69 In other words, this is not a gradual approach but a direct counter-measure against inveterate self-cherishing.

70 The practice described below, however, does contain many elements of the sevenfold cause-and-effect practice.

71 Literally here, the *brahmāvihāras* (Tib. *tshangs pa'i gnas*), this refers to love, compassion, joy, and equanimity.

72 The text says "black light."

73 See Patrul Rinpoche 1994: 224–26. "Daughter" was the name of the Buddha in one of his former incarnations. Born as the son of a sea captain called Vallabha, he was given the name Daughter as a form of protection, as all his parents' previous sons had died. Later in life, when on a voyage, he witnessed the suffering that comes, as a result of karma, to those who have abused their mothers from the past, and he vowed to free beings from such pain by taking it all upon himself.

74 This quotation is from his mind-training text, which appears in *Mind Training: The Great Collection*. See Jinpa 2006: 269.

75 A powerful god who tempts and obstructs us on the path to enlightenment.

76 The commitment referred to here is the practice of taking refuge and relying on the Buddha, Dharma, and Saṅgha. In the Mahāyāna this too comes from love.

77 In this context *dhāraṇī* signifies an infallible memory.

78 *Tsho ba mgre ba.* The word *mgre ba* may be an error. (KAR)

79 (1) The guests invited out of respect, the Three Jewels; (2) the guests invited on account of their qualities, the Dharma protectors; (3) the guests invited out of compassion, the beings of the six classes; and (4) the guests to whom we owe karmic debts.

80 The text only gives the first line here.

81 This is quoted in Śāntideva's *Śikṣāsamuccaya.*

82 Read *tshong 'dus* for *tshong dus.* (KAR)

83 Also quoted in *Śikṣāsamuccaya.*

84 See note 61 above.

85 Pratyekabuddhas and śrāvakas are followers of the basic vehicle, who strive to escape the suffering of saṃsāra and attain the level of an arhat. The former are said to achieve this goal by themselves, without the aid of a teacher.

86 Harmful influences (Tib. *gdon*) are described as spirits or forces that are helpful when they are given offerings but harmful when they are not.

87 *Yakṣas* are semidivine spirits who possess magical powers and are associated with forests. Although mostly benevolent, their Tibetan name (*gnod sbyin*), which literally means "harm-bringer," suggests they also have a malignant side.

88 *Gandharvas* (literally "scent eaters") are spirits who feed on odors.

89 *Mahoragas,* or "great uragas," are giant serpent-like creatures.

90 See note 72 above.

91 Following Jinpa (2006), an alternative translation of the title would be *Aspiration of Granting the Gift of Loving Kindness.*

92 This is an especially powerful method for beginners. You can even count with a mala as you recite slogans such as "May all beings have happiness and its causes." (KAR) In the past, there was once a Kadampa master who meditated on impermanence. When he reflected on how the time of death is uncertain, he realized the uselessness of actions focused on this life, and picking up his *mālā,* he recited over and over again, "Useless, useless, useless...." (Khenpo Appey 2011: 10).

93 Virūpa. See Jinpa 2006: 612nn409–10.

94 Reference not found.

95 *Mtha' bral dbu ma chen po'i gdams pa zab don rab gsal.*

96 This could refer to the vows of individual liberation (*prātimokṣa*) and of the bodhisattvas, or to the vows of ordained people and lay people. See Dalai Lama 2001: 96.

97 The text says "without the thorns of enemies" (*dgra'i tsher ma med pa*), but we

are reading it as *sgra'i tsher ma med pa*. Sharma (1997: 59) has "without a jarring tone."

98 According to Jinpa (2006: 640n870), this is from the *Commentary on the Difficult Points of "Lamp for the Path to Enlightenment."*

99 The last two lines do not seem actually to appear in Śāntideva's text.

100 The *four māras* are the māra of the psychophysical aggregates, the māra of the destructive emotions, the māra of the Lord of Death, and the māra of the sons of the gods.

101 Tormas (*gtor ma*) are ritual cakes, usually made from dough, and often decorated elaborately with colorful butter sculptures.

102 *Dhāraṇīs* are mantras, usually quite long, condensing particular teachings, or even entire sūtras, into (potentially) memorizable forms.

103 The Tibetan here says *chos bzhi pa'i mdo*, and although there are two sūtras by that name in the Dergé Kangyur, this quote actually comes from the *Chos bzhi bstan pa'i mdo* (Skt. *Caturdharmanirdeśasūtra*).

104 The masters of sickness (*nad bdag*) are malevolent spirits.

105 This and the following two lines do not appear in standard editions of the *Seven Points*, as in, for example, Jinpa 2006.

106 From *Teachings on the Qualities of Mañjuśrī's Pure Land*, chapter 18 of the *Ratnakūṭa Sūtra*.

107 The *transference of consciousness*, or *powa* (*'pho ba*), is a practice for the moment of death, through which one's own or another's consciousness can be transferred to a pure realm.

108 Note that these instructions are given from a male perspective. For females, the posture is reversed because of the different position of the subtle channels.

109 The text is saying that while following the mind training, we should not neglect the precepts of the Basic Vehicle, which almost exclusively deal with actions of body and speech.

110 Powerful trees might be inhabited by gods and powerful lakes by nāgas. Ordinarily to desecrate their abodes would induce sickness. (KAR)

111 For example, a good-natured person will keep in mind all the benefit they have received, no matter when it occurred, without forgetting it. In a similar way, we might harbor resentment, keeping in mind all the harms that have been done to us and never forgetting them. The meaning here is that we should not hold on to things for a long time in that sense. In other words, we should not bear grudges. (KAR)

112 Literally "the armor of impetus," corresponding to the first of the five strengths.

113 Literally "like grass at a crossroads," this refers to grass that has been used, trampled, and scattered around and is consequently of little value.

114 The original text contained an extra word that is no longer legible, as indicated by an ellipsis in the recent edition. As a result, the meaning of this line is ambiguous.

115 One of Ga Rabjampa's alternative names. It is not clear from his biography when or from whom he acquired this name.

Bibliography

❦

Texts Cited by the Author

Sutras and tantras

Aspiration of Maitrāyajña (Tib. *Byams pa mchod sbyin gyi smon lam*).

Aspiration to Supreme Conduct (Skt. *Agracaryāpraṇidhāna*; Tib. *Mchog gi spyod pa'i smon lam*).

Chapter of the Truthful One (Tib. *Bden pa po'i le'u*).

Cloud of Jewels Sūtra (Skt. *Ratnamegha-sūtra*; Tib. *Mdo sde dkon mchog sprin*).

Collection of Meaningful Expressions (Skt. *Udānavarga*; Tib. *Ched du brjod pa'i tshoms*).

Compendium of Dharma Sūtra (Skt. *Dharmasaṃgīti-sūtra*; Tib. *Chos yang dag par sdud pa'i mdo*).

Dhāraṇi of Infinite Gateways (Skt. *Anantamukhanirhāra-dhāraṇī*; Tib. *Sgo mtha' yas pa'i gzungs*).

Gaṇḍavyūha Sūtra (Tib. *Sdong po bkod pa'i mdo*).

Great Parinirvāṇa Sūtra (Skt. *Mahāparinirvāṇa-sūtra*; Tib. *Myang 'das chen po'i mdo*).

Hundred Actions (Skt. *Karmaśataka*; Tib. *Las brgya pa*).

Jātakas (Tib. *Skyes rabs*).

King of Samādhi Sūtra (Skt. *Samādhirāja-sūtra*; Tib. *Ting nge 'dzin rgyal po'i mdo*).

Lalitavistara Sūtra (Tib. *Rgya cher rol pa*).

Mañjuśrī Root Tantra (Tib. *'Jam dpal rtsa ba'i rgyud*).

Moon Lamp Sūtra (Skt. *Candrapradīpa*; Tib. *Zla ba sgron me'i mdo*), an alternative name for the *King of Samādhi Sūtra.*

Precious Verse Summary of the Perfection of Wisdom. See *Verse Summary of the Perfection of Wisdom.*

Samantabhadra's Prayer of Good Actions (Tib. *Bzang spyod smon lam*).

Śūraṅgama Sūtra (Tib. *Dpa' bar 'gro ba'i mdo*).

Sūtra of Akṣayamati (Skt. *Akṣayamatinirdeśa-sūtra*; Tib. *Blo gros mi zad pas bstan pa'i mdo*).

Sūtra of Completely Pure Conduct (Tib. *Spyod yul yongs dag gi mdo*). Chapter 16 of the *Avataṃsaka Sūtra.*

Sūtra of Four Dharmas (Skt. *Caturdharmanirdeśa-sūtra*; Tib. *Chos bzhi bstan pa'i mdo*).

Sūtra of the Vajra Banner of Victory (Skt. *Vajraketu-sūtra*; Tib. *Rdo rje rgyal mtshan gyi mdo*).

Sūtra of the Application of Mindfulness (Tib. *Dran pa nyer bzhag gi mdo*).

Sūtra of Instructions to the King (Skt. *Rājāvavādaka-sūtra*; Tib. *Rgyal po la gdams pa'i mdo*).

Sūtra of the Secret of the Tathāgatas (Skt. *Tathāgatācintyaguhyanirdeśa-sūtra*; Tib. *De bzhin gshegs pa'i gsang ba'i mdo*).

Sūtra on Impermanence (Skt. *Anityatā-sūtra*; Tib. *Mi rtag pa nyid kyi mdo*).

Sūtra Requested by Nārāyaṇa (Skt. *Nārāyaṇaparipṛcchā-sūtra*; Tib. *Sred med kyi bus zhus pa'i mdo*).

Sūtra Requested by the Sovereign Lord of Dhāraṇīs (Skt. *Dhāraṇīśvara-rāja-sūtra*; Tib. *Gzungs kyi dbang phyug rgyal pos zhus pa'i mdo*).

Sūtra Requested by Vīradatta (Skt. *Vīradattagṛhapatiparipṛcchā-sūtra*; Tib. *Dpa' sbyin gyis zhus pa'i mdo*).

Verse Summary of the Perfection of Wisdom (Skt. *Prajñāpāramitā-sañcayagāthā*; Tib. *Shes rab kyi pha rol tu phyin pa sdud pa tshigs su bcad pa*).

Treatises

Āryadeva. *Four Hundred Verses* (Skt. *Catuḥśataka*; Tib. *Bzhi brgya pa*).

Aśvaghoṣa. *Fifty Stanzas on Following a Teacher* (Skt. *Gurupañcāśikā*; Tib. *Bla ma lnga bcu pa*).

_____. *Letter of Consolation* (Skt. *Śokavinodana*; Tib. *Myan ngan bsal ba'i springs yig*).

Atiśa. *Lamp for the Path to Enlightenment* (Skt. *Bodhipathapradīpa*; Tib. *Byang chub lam sgron*).

Bhāvaviveka. *Heart of the Middle Way* (Skt. *Madhyamakahṛdaya*; Tib. *Dbu ma'i snying po*).

Candragomin. *Letter to a Disciple* (Skt. *Śiṣyalekha*; Tib. *Slob spring*).

Candrakīrti. *Introduction to the Middle Way* (Skt. *Madhyamakāvatāra*; Tib. *Dbu ma la 'jug pa*).

Dharmakīrti. *Commentary on Valid Cognition* (Skt. *Pramāṇavārttika*; Tib. *Tshad ma rnam 'grel*).

Kamalaśīla. *Stages of Meditation II* (Skt. *Bhāvanākrama*; Tib. *Sgom rim bar pa*).

Maitreya. *Distinguishing the Middle from Extremes* (Skt. *Madhyānta-vibhāga*; Tib. *Dbus mtha' rnam 'byed*).

_____. *Ornament of Clear Realization* (Skt. *Abhisamayālaṃkāra*; Tib. *Mngon rtogs rgyan*).

_____. *Ornament of Mahāyāna Sūtras* (Skt. *Māhayānasūtrālaṃkāra*; Tib. *Mdo sde rgyan*).

_____. *Sublime Continuum* (Skt. *Uttaratantra*; Tib. *Rgyud bla ma*).

Nāgārjuna. *Letter to a Friend* (Skt. *Suhṛllekha*; Tib. *Bshes spring*).

_____. *Precious Garland* (Skt. *Ratnāvalī*; Tib. *Rin chen phreng ba*).

Sakya Paṇḍitā. *Clear Differentiation of the Three Sets of Vows* (Tib. *Sdom gsum rab dbye*).

Śāntideva. *Compendium of Training* (Skt. *Śikṣāsamuccaya*; Tib. *Bslab pa kun btus*).

_____. *Introduction to the Bodhisattva's Way of Life* (Skt. *Bodhi-caryāvatāra*; Tib. *spyod 'jug*).

Vasubandhu. *Advice for the Assembly* (Skt. *Sambhāraparikathā*; Tib. *Tshogs kyi gtam*).

———. *Treasury of Abhidharma* (Skt. *Abhidharmakośa*; Tib. *Mngon pa mdzod*).

Translator's Bibliography

Cleary, Thomas. *The Flower Ornament Scripture: A Translation of the Avatamsaka Sutra*. Boston: Shambhala, 1993.

Conze, Edward. *The Perfection of Wisdom in Eight Thousand Lines and Its Verse Summary*. Bolinas, CA: 1973. Reprinted Delhi: Sri Satguru, 1994.

Dalai Lama, The. *Stages of Meditation*. Venerable Geshe Lobsang Jordhen, Losang Choephel Ganchenpa, and Jeremy Russell, trans. Ithaca: Snow Lion, 2001.

Dilgo Khyentse Rinpoche. *Enlightened Courage*. Padmakara Translation Group, trans. Ithaca: Snow Lion, 2006.

Dreyfus, Georges. *The Sound of Two Hands Clapping*. Berkeley and Los Angeles: University of California Press, 2003.

Ga Rabjampa Künga Yeshé. Sga rab 'byams pa kun dga' ye shes kyi gsung 'bum [Collected Works]. Unknown publisher, 2005.

Jackson, David P. *The Early Abbots of 'Phan-po Na-lendra: The Vicissitudes of a Great Tibetan Monastery in the 15th Century*. Wiener Studien zur Tibetologie und Budhismuskunde 23. Vienna: Arbeitskreis für tibetische und buddhistische Studien, Universität Wien, 1989.

———. *A Saint in Seattle: The Life of the Tibetan Mystic Dezhung Rinpoche*. Boston: Wisdom, 2003.

Jamgön Kongtrul. *The Great Path of Awakening*. Ken McLeod, trans. Shambhala, 2005.

———. *The Treasury of Knowledge, Book Six, Part Three: Frameworks of Buddhist Philosophy*. Kalu Rinpoché Translation Group, trans. Ithaca: Snow Lion, 2007.

Jinpa, Thupten, trans. *Mind Training: The Great Collection*. Boston: Wisdom, 2006.

Khenpo Appey. *Blo sbyong don bdun ma'i bka' khrid*. Kathmandu: International Buddhist Academy, 2011.

La Vallée-Poussin, Louis de, trans. *Abhidharmakośabhāṣyam*, 4 vols. Leo Pruden, trans. Fremont, CA: Asian Humanities Press, 1988.

Maitreyanatha/Āryāsaṅga. *The Universal Vehicle Discourse Literature.* L. Jamspal, R. Clark, J. Wilson, L. Zwilling, M. Sweet, and R. Thurman, trans. New York: American Institute of Buddhist Studies, 2004.

Martin, Dan. *TibSkrit Philology*, revised 2011 (available online).

Mātṛceṭa and Candragomin. *Invitation to Enlightenment.* Michael Hahn, trans. Berkeley: Dharma Publishing, 1999.

Nāgārjuna. *The Precious Garland: An Epistle to a King.* John Dunne and Sara McClintock, trans. Boston: Wisdom, 1997.

Padmakara Translation Group. *Nagarjuna's Letter to a Friend with Commentary by Kangyur Rinpoche.* Ithaca: Snow Lion, 2005.

Patrul Rinpoche. *The Words of My Perfect Teacher.* Padmakara Translation Group, trans. Boston and London: Shambhala, 1994. (2nd edition, 1998.)

Ringu Tulku. *Mind Training.* Ithaca: Snow Lion, 2007.

———. *The Ri-Mé Philosophy of Jamgön Kongtrul the Great.* Boston: Shambhala, 2006.

Sakya Pandita Kunga Gyaltshen. *A Clear Differentiation of the Three Codes.* Jared Rhoton, trans. Albany: State University of New York Press, 2002.

Sharma, Parmananda. *Bhāvanākrama of Kamalaśīla.* New Delhi: Aditya Prakashan, 1997.

Smith, E. Gene. *Among Tibetan Texts.* Boston: Wisdom, 2001.

Sogyal Rinpoche. *The Tibetan Book of Living and Dying*, rev. ed. San Francisco: HarperSanFrancisco, 2002.

Sopa, Geshe Lhundub. *Peacock in the Poison Grove.* Michael J. Sweet and Leonard Zwilling, trans. Boston: Wisdom, 2001.

Trungpa, Chögyam. *Training the Mind and Cultivating Loving Kindness.* Boston: Shambhala, 1993.

Van Schaik, Sam. *Tibet: A History.* New Haven and London: Yale University Press, 2011.

Zhechen Gyaltsab Gyurmed Padma Namgyal. *Path of Heroes: Birth of Enlightenment*, 2 vols. Berkeley: Dharma Publishing, 1995.

Index

About Rigpa Translations

———— ✺ ————

Rigpa Translations is a group of modern-day lotsawas working under the guidance of Sogyal Rinpoche and the mentorship of senior editor Patrick Gaffney to translate important teachings from Tibetan into English and other languages. Visit us on the web at www.rigpatranslations.org for more translations and resources on Tibetan Buddhism.

About Wisdom Publications

❧ ❦

Wisdom Publications is dedicated to offering works relating to and inspired by Buddhist traditions.

To learn more about us or to explore our other books, please visit our website at www.wisdompubs.org.

You can subscribe to our e-newsletter or request our print catalog online, or by writing to:

Wisdom Publications
199 Elm Street
Somerville, Massachusetts 02144 USA

You can also contact us at 617-776-7416, or info@wisdompubs.org.

Wisdom is a nonprofit, charitable 501(c)(3) organization and donations in support of our mission are tax deductible.

Wisdom Publications is affiliated with the Foundation for the Preservation of the Mahayana Tradition (FPMT).